ML Primer

RYAN STANSIFER

University of North Texas

PRENTICE HALL, Englewood Cliffs, New Jersey 07632

Library of Congress Cataloging-in-Publication Data

Stansifer, Ryan
    ML primer / Ryan Stansifer.
        p.   cm.
    Includes bibliographical references and index.
    ISBN 0-13-561721-9
    1. ML (Computer program language) 2. Functional programming
(Computer science)   I. Title.
QA76.73.M6S73 1992
005.13'3--dc20   91-43146
                                                        CIP

Acquisitions Editor/Editor-in-Chief: Marcia Horton
Production Editor: Bayani Mendoza de Leon
Cover Designer: Ben Santora
Prepress Buyer: Linda Behrens
Manufacturing Buyer: Dave Dickey
Copy Editor: Andrea Hammer
Editorial Assistant: Diana Penha

The author and publisher of this book have used their best efforts in preparing
this book. These efforts include the development, research, and testing
of the theories and programs to determine their effectiveness. The author
and publisher make no warranty of any kind, expressed or implied, with regard
to these programs or the documentation contained in this book. The author
and publisher shall not be liable in any event for incidental or consequential
damages in connection with, or arising out of, the furnishing, performance,
or use of these programs.

Printed in the United States of America

10 9 8 7 6 5 4 3 2 1

ISBN 0-13-561721-9

TRADEMARK INFORMATION

Miranda is a trademark of Research Software Ltd.

Unix is a registered trademark of AT&T (Bell Laboratories).

T$_E$X is a trademark of American Mathematical Society.

Prentice-Hall International (UK) Limited, *London*
Prentice-Hall of Australia Pty. Limited, *Sydney*
Prentice-Hall Canada Inc., *Toronto*
Prentice-Hall Hispanoamericana, S.A., *Mexico*
Prentice-Hall of India Private Limited, *New Delhi*
Prentice-Hall of Japan, Inc., *Tokyo*
Simon & Schuster Asia Pte. Ltd., *Singapore*
Editora Prentice-Hall do Brasil, Ltda., *Rio de Janeiro*

Contents

Preface

In this book we introduce the programming language ML. We have tried to keep the approach succinct to appeal to those who have heard about ML and want to learn about it, and who may not be able to invest a large effort to do so. We have also tried to keep the discussion simple with lots of examples to appeal to those who may be learning a functional language for the first time.

Our goal is to introduce strongly typed, functional languages to a wide audience. The reader should have little difficulty in moving from the introduction of ML here to other similar languages like Haskell or Miranda. All languages are influenced by their history, standardization efforts, and implementation efforts. We try to remain faithful to the standard as promulgated in *The Definition of Standard ML* [12]. Properly we must speak of the language Standard ML to distinguish it from other variants. We call the language ML for short, however.

We have tried not to get involved with the details of one particular implementation. There are several implementations for ML. A very important one is being developed primarily by David MacQueen and Andrew Appel [1], and is called Standard ML of New Jersey (SML of NJ). Another one is CAML-Light [10]. This implementation runs on PC's. User interaction with each different system is unique, and so some implementation details are unavoidable. We have described the basic ML system we have developed. But this should prove to be no impediment to using this book as a guide to any of the implementations of the language.

This book does not attempt to justify and explain all aspects of functional programming. This would detract from the primary goal of describing one particular functional language. Several lengthy treatments have already been written [5, 8, 14]. Those who want to learn about functional languages are invited to read this book and try programming in ML. They may then be convinced to study such languages further or to use functional languages in their applications.

Data structures, or types, are of central importance to ML. We have devoted a chapter (chapter 7) to the subject. Some more difficult material appears there, especially the last two sections. This material is not essential to program in ML but does provide a basis for further study of this fascinating topic.

We have not provided a thorough discussion of modules. Although modules deserve a more lengthy treatment, they are not necessary to appreciate a strong typed, functional language, of which ML is a sterling example. Furthermore, the ML system described here does not attempt to implement them.

A collection of the most directly relevant material is listed in the bibliography. The bibliography should serve as a guide to further study. This book also has an index and a glossary to help it serve as a reference to the language. Some exercises are included to stimulate programming activity with the language. These exercises are placed at the end of the book, because most interesting problems require chapter 4 on functions and chapter 5 on user-defined data structures as a prerequisite.

Our thanks go to the reviewers selected by Prentice Hall, Monagur Muralidharan, University of Iowa, and Carl A. Gunter, University of Pennsylvania, as well as James Sasaki, University of Maryland Baltimore County, who helped in the review process and who offered suggestions for the manuscript's improvement.

Ryan Stansifer

■ Chapter 1

Introduction

The programming language ML was originally designed for use as the metalanguage in the Logic for Computable Functions (LCF) verification system [6]. Hence the source of the name for the language, ML for Meta-Language. Despite its origins in the 1980s as a language for a specific purpose, it is a versatile language. A language standard has emerged [12]. ML is a strongly typed, functional programming language with a natural syntax and just a few primitive concepts.

1.1 SALIENT FEATURES

The distinctive features of ML are the following:

- Pattern matching
- Exception handling
- Type inference
- Polymorphism
- Recursive data structures

Pattern matching is a relatively novel generalization of traditional parameter association by position. Exception handling is a general mechanism to program special cases without harming the structure of the program for the usual cases. The last three features concern data structures.

The structure of data types in ML is the single most innovative and appealing feature of ML. There are several aspects of types that are important.

1

First, the types of all[1] identifiers are inferred from their use. Thus, declaring the types of identifiers is redundant. Second, a function definition applies to as many data structures as possible. Only the minimum structure as actually required in the definition is assumed about the data structure of the input. Third, recursive data structures, like trees, are permitted. This eliminates many uses of pointers. As pointers are error prone, recursive data structures are a valuable tool in managing software development.

Standard ML [12] has a sophisticated mechanism for modules using the **signature** and **structure** constructs. These are described briefly in chapter 9.

1.2 FUNCTIONAL PROGRAMMING

We have said ML is a functional programming language. In a functional language function application is the primary means used to compute. This is in contrast to conventional languages (sometimes called imperative languages) such as FORTRAN, Pascal, C, Ada, and so on in which the programmer accomplishes a task by moving data around in memory cells called variables. In such languages the flow of control is arranged to cause the correct sequence of assignment statements to be executed.

Here, for example, is the factorial program written in Pascal.

```
function fact (n: integer): integer;
    var p: integer;
begin
    p := 1;
    while (n > 1) do
    begin
        p := p * n;
        n := n-1;
    end;
    fact := p;
end;
```

This program causes the assignment **p:=p*n** to be executed the correct number of times to leave the proper value in the variable **p**.

All good programmers immediately scrutinize a function definition in a conventional language for several possible defects that often crop up in imperative programming:

- Is the argument passed by creating a reference to the variable containing the actual argument and not by copying the value? If so, the assignment to the variable **n** may inadvertently change the value of the actual argument.

---

[1] Well, almost all. See section 7.4 on overloading.

- Does the function assign a new value to any nonlocal variable? If so, the function does more than compute the factorial function—it has a hidden effect on the values of other variables.
- Do any two variable names refer to the same location? If so, an assignment to one changes the value of the other.

These pitfalls are due to the particular realization of computation in which cells of memory are modified in a sequence controlled by the instruction counter. This fundamental model of a computing device (which also includes storing the program in memory) is often called the *von Neuman machine* in honor of the computing pioneer John von Neuman who contributed both to the theory and hardware of traditional computing machinery.

The functional programming paradigm realizes computation in a manner that is not directly related to the actual operation of most computers. A more functional version of the Pascal **fact** program can be written as follows:

```
function fact (n: integer): integer;
begin
    if (n > 1) then
      fact := n^fact (n-1)
    else
      fact := 1
end
```

In this version, the **while** statement has been replaced by recursion. The function **fact** calls itself. A **while** statement can be implemented directly on a von Neuman machine by changing the program counter, whereas implementing recursion on machines of conventional architecture is more difficult as it requires the maintenance of a run-time stack of records for each invocation of a function. But all programs written using a **while** statement can be written using recursion. In fact, recursive functions can compute anything that could be computed using assignments and **while** statements. In the functional paradigm the problem is decomposed into pieces that are computed by functions, and these results are then combined by a function into the final answer. In the case of the factorial function, we take advantage of the fact that we can compute the factorial of n easily, if we know the factorial of $n - 1$. This is, for programmers, easier to understand.

The advantage of the functional programming paradigm lies in the decreased reliance on side effects. This makes programs easier to write, understand, and to reason about. The term "easier" is a relative notion that is difficult to quantify. Clearly, if one is familiar and comfortable with the von Neuman machine, thinking about computation in any other way may not be any easier.

The disadvantage of the functional programming paradigm is that the programmer can no longer obtain the most efficient representation of the program on a machine with conventional architecture. The term "efficient" is also a relative notion. Saving 10s of bytes and 10s of instructions in the age of 24-megabyte memories and 25-million-instructions-per-second machines is not as important as it once was. Furthermore, the technology to implement functional languages on conventional machine architectures has improved markedly as the use of these languages becomes more widespread.

The theoretical basis of functional programming has its origins in the lambda calculus of Alonzo Church. The lambda calculus was proposed as a theoretical model of computation in the same manner that Alan Turing proposed Turing machines. Turing machines are uninspiring as a means of expressing computation, however, and bear no useful relation to programming, imperative or otherwise. Conversely, the lambda calculus captures the commonality of the functional programming paradigm. Thus the study of the lambda calculus is essential for further study about functional programming.

ML is not the only functional programming language. The oldest and most widely known functional language is LISP, developed in the 1960s by John McCarthy. LISP is famous for its sparse syntax, its representation of both data and programs as lists, and its typeless approach. Other functional programming languages include Scheme, which is a modern dialect of LISP, Haskell, which is a typed language with lazy evaluation, and FP, which has a fixed set of ways to combine functions to define new functions.

1.3 TYPES IN PROGRAMMING

The approach that ML takes to types, in particular Milner style **let**-polymorphism [10], is what makes ML different from other functional programming languages.

Each programming language has a collection of different sorts of values that are the objects of computation, values like integers and boolean values, for instance. These values are stored in the hardware, divided up among the basic cells or words of the machine's memory. The operations of addition on integers or logical negation are translated into instructions that manipulate words in the computer memory. If the programmer causes boolean values to be added together like integers, it is possible that the machine will manipulate the unmarked words computing, possibly, the wrong answer. Or even worse, the answer may be right most of the time, only failing at the worst possible moment many months after the program was written. Applying an operation to an argument whose intended interpretation is a value of a type not appropriate for the operation is a type error.

Certain applications, say systems programming, may require that the programmer be aware of the representation in the hardware of the values in the language and even operate directly on uninterpreted words of memory.

However, programs that take advantage of the representation of data are often hard to read and difficult to port to different machines. (It should not be overlooked that systems programs may require the representation of data in small portions of the program that might well be isolated. This is the approach of "unsafe" modules in the programming language Modula 3.) So it is reasonable to ask that a language require that such type errors be caught and reported.

One possible approach to catching type errors is to keep track of the types of all the values and check to see if any operation inappropriately accesses a value during the execution of the program. This approach is called dynamic or run-time type checking. Done naively, dynamic type checking can be exorbitantly expensive. The type of each word of memory must itself be stored somewhere. Every operation must check the type of the arguments (this could take more instructions than the operation itself). Of course, a good translator or compiler would observe that many of the checks are unnecessary and omit the tests. In general, it is impossible to remove all the tests.

Another approach is to have the compiler report any operation that might possibly result in a type error. The advantage of this approach is the programmer is warned when the program is being written that there could be a problem. A program that escapes this scrutiny unscathed will not have a run-time type error. But how many programs would squeeze through?

Here language design can play a role. The right collection of types and the right organization of functions will permit the types of all values to be predicted in advance by the compiler. This enables the compiler to do the type checking, and this is called static or compile-time type checking. A language that permits the compiler to do all the type checking is said to be strongly typed. ML and Ada are examples of strongly typed languages. The programming languages APL, C, and LISP are not.

It is important to select the types in the language carefully. Some gerrymandering is required to make the problem tractable for the compiler. For example, what is the type of the division operator? We may want to claim that the type of quotient is any nonzero integer to avoid dividing by zero. It is more convenient, however, to take the type of the quotient to be an integer. Thus dividing by zero is not a "type" error, but a run-time anomaly of a different sort. It is possible to design a language that makes these anomalies (1) relatively rare, (2) errors that must (and can) be detected, (3) efficient to test in the hardware, (4) require no (or little) overhead in the usual case, and (5) entirely in the control of the programmer. Different languages may choose different boundaries between the compile-time notion of a type and the legal values at run time. For example, the legality of variant records in Ada is checked at run time, in ML the equivalent data structures are checked at compile time.

We now consider further the purpose and promise of a compile-time notion of a type. It is possible that a collection of types that the compiler finds easy to demonstrate the lack of type errors may not be a collection that is appealing to the programmer. Instead we argue that types are a useful programming construct for the following three reasons:

1. Types reduce the use of pointers.
2. Types provide a partial specification.
3. Types help manage complexity.

Just as functions are a good way of handling the flow of control in a computation, the right type system is helpful in organizing data. Recursive types permit the introduction of complex data structures without the use of pointers. Pointers are often error prone and confusing. It has been argued that pointers are the "goto" of data structures [7], because they require the programmer to think about the low-level implementation of the data structures. Here is an example of a binary tree as it would be written in Pascal.

```
type
    ptr  = ^ node;  { pointer to a node }
    node = record
        info: integer;
        llink, rlink: ptr
    end;
```

Here is the same data structure implemented in ML.

```
datatype Tree = empty | node of int * Tree * Tree;
```

It is shorter, but, more important, the distinction between a **node** and a pointer to a **node** is no longer necessary. It is also a "natural" definition for a tree. One could treat a tree as a special case of a graph and represent it as an adjacency matrix. In the programming language APL one would be forced into this approach. Only the most ardent algebraist would find this approach more natural.

Practical experience shows that even the most mundane collection of types provides a useful sanity check on the stream of consciousness that the programmer pours into a program. For example, it is quite easy in languages with list data structures to confuse concatenating an element onto a list with appending two lists together. Such mistakes elicit compile-time errors in ML but cause no problems in LISP until (if ever) some inscrutable run-time error occurs. Thus, types in ML allow the language to perform an internal consistency check. Moreover, the types provide a weak specification of the functions in ML. A function for traversing an integer binary tree cannot be inadvertently used on binary trees with string-valued data—the compiler will not permit it. The compiler verifies that the input has the correct type for the program.

More than specification, types may be the way to manage complexity [3]. Certainly large programs are a source of much frustration in the modern world of financial transactions, air traffic control, weather forecasting, space exploration, and medical imagery to name just some applications. No one, and certainly no one *small*, example will be convincing that ML types are useful in managing complexity. We offer an example anyway. We give an abstract, hence quite general, binary tree. We are suggesting that the type system in ML makes it possible for the programmer to handle complex objects more easily than in some languages.

```
datatype 'a Tree = empty | node of 'a * 'a Tree * 'a Tree;
```

This tree structure is appropriate for more binary trees, not just those with integer information in the nodes. It is just as easy in ML to write a traversal function, say, for this data structure as the other one. In Pascal, this generality is difficult to accomplish. Even in Ada in which this generality is possible, the programmer is required to master new and strange constructs (i.e., generics) to accomplish this.

The type system in ML is a useful mechanism for organizing complex data in a natural way; however, it is not adequate for large applications. For this reason, a module construct is part of Standard ML [12]. These and other sophisticated type constructs are being explored to make types useful for solving the problems of programming-in-the-large. Whatever success is obtained in harnessing computers to solve complex problems, it is likely that types will play a significant part.

■ Chapter 2

The Basics

In this chapter we introduce the essentials of the ML programming language. The material in this chapter is enough to gain a feeling for the language and to survive an initial session with the ML system. We describe the interaction with the system, the fundamental objects and operations in ML, and the nature and form of error messages that occur when things go wrong.

2.1 INTERACTION WITH THE ML SYSTEM

ML is an interactive programming language. An ML session consists of a dialog between the user and the system. The user enters a phrase terminated by a semicolon. Then the ML system parses the input, analyzes it, compiles it, executes it, and prints a response. Schematically the interaction looks like this:

ML> *phrase* ;
    response

ML prompts the user for a phrase with the characters "**ML>**" and responds on the following line. A phrase entered in response to the "**ML>**" prompt is said to be at the *top level*. A *session* consists of several phrase and response pairs beginning after the invocation of the ML system and terminated by typing a control-D to the system.

One legal phrase the user may enter is an expression. The system's response is the value of the expression and its type. The dialog takes the following form:

ML> *expression ;*
   value : type

For example, **17** is a legal ML expression. Entering this into the system after the prompt and terminating the line with a semicolon yields the following dialog:

ML> 17;
   17 : int

The ML system evaluates the expression. In the case of **17**, the expression evaluates to itself. The type of the expression **17** is integer, which the ML system indicates by printing **int** after the colon. ML infers the type of each expression. For complex expressions, the type is a useful summary of the expression, providing a check as to whether the programmer has created the intended object or not.

The following simple arithmetic expressions evaluate to the obvious answers.

ML> 2+3;
   5 : int

ML> 7-4;
   3 : int

Extra white space (strings of blanks, tabs, and newline characters) does not have any effect on the meaning of an ML expression. This permits the programmer to use white space to enhance the legibility of programs. All white space has the same effect as a single blank. Thus a newline character, ten blanks, or twenty tabs can be replaced by a single blank. In some cases the white space can be removed altogether. Thus, the following three expressions are identical:

ML> 5 *   **3**   **;**
   15 : int

ML> 5 * 3 ;
   15 : int

ML> 5*3;
   15 : int

Since the newline character has the same effect as a blank, an expression can be spread across more than one line, if desired. Because of this, the final semicolon is needed to recognize that the expression is complete.

```
ML> 6
..> -4
..> ;
   2 : int
```

Without the semicolon, typing the character **6** on a line by itself, as in the preceding example, would not unambiguously communicate the user's intent. It might indicate that the expression consisting of a single digit is to be evaluated, or that the expression continues on the next line. Thus, the semicolon is needed to terminate an expression.

The ML system gives a prompt when expecting input. After the first line the prompt is "**..>**" indicating that more input is expected or required to form a complete phrase.

It is not necessary to input an expression singly. More than one expression can be given on an input line.

```
ML> 2+5; 6-4;
   7 : int
   2 : int
```

Whether or not multiple expressions are entered on one or more lines, the ML system responds to each expression individually on a separate line.

Comments are permitted anywhere between tokens of the language. In ML comments begin with the two-character sequence **(***, and they end with the two-character sequence ***)**.

```
ML> ~3;          (* A negative number *)
   ~3 : int

ML> ~ 7;         (* ~ is the unary negation operator *)
   ~7 : int
```

Nested comments are permitted so that whole sections of code can be "commented out" in a convenient fashion.

2.2 BASIC DATA TYPES

ML has a rich collection of data types. We can divide the collection of data types into three categories.

1. There are the basic data types. ML has five basic data types: integer, string, boolean, real, and unit. In this section we will look at the literals and operations on these five basic types.

2. There are the structured data types. Type operators combine types to form structured, or compound, types. In the next section we talk about three built-in type operators: tuples, records, and lists. There is another built-in type operator for functions. Because functions are so important, chapter 4 is devoted to them. A fifth built-in type operator is for pointers, and it is discussed in chapter 8.

3. There are user-defined types. The user-defined data types are reminiscent of variant record types found in other programming languages. Typically variant records are not used much in other programming languages, but user-defined types are quite important to programming in ML. They are quite general and encompass enumerated types. User-defined data types are discussed in chapter 5.

The preceding list of data types does not mention arrays, which are quite common in other programming languages. This deserves some explanation. In a functional language like ML, arrays are problematic. The implementation of functional languages usually requires values to be copied often. For large arrays this is expensive. It is to be expected that particular implementations of ML may offer arrays or other built-in data types and type operators.

2.2.1 Integer

We have already seen examples of integer literals. These are written in the usual way. Negative integers are written using the unary negation operator, which is denoted by the ASCII character ~. The four usual arithmetic operations are available in ML. Here is an example using addition, subtraction and multiplication.

```
ML> 2+3; 4-5; 6*7;
    5 : int
   ~1 : int
   42 : int
```

The character − is used exclusively for the binary subtraction operator. This should not be confused with ~, which is used for the unary negation operator. There is a slight difference between ~5, which is an integer literal, and ~ 5, which is an expression in which the operation ~ is applied to the integer literal 5. Division for the integers works by having two operations, one for finding the quotient and one for finding the remainder.

```
ML> 37 div 5; 37 mod 5;
    7 : int
    2 : int
```

The precise definition of these two operators is given by the requirement that the values $r = a$ **mod** d and $q = a$ **div** d satisfy the condition $d * q + r = a$, where either $0 \leq r < d$ or $d < r \leq 0$. Thus, if the divisor is negative, so is the remainder (when it is not zero).

```
ML> ~37 mod 5;
    ~2 : int
```

The ML language gives an implementation-independent definition of **mod**, unlike the C definition of %, which is implementation dependent. This definition of **mod** is identical to the Ada definition of **rem**.

The unary operator **abs** is also predefined. It computes the absolute value of integers.

There is no limit on the magnitude of integers. As a practical matter, integer literals are limited to about eighty digits, because that is the size of the largest allowable token.

```
ML> 299792500;          (* velocity of light in a vacuum (m/sec) *)
    299792500 : int
```

Some implementations of ML limit the magnitude of integers.

The associativity and the precedence of the arithmetic operations follow general mathematical usage. When associativity is in doubt, parentheses can be used.

2.2.2 String

Strings in ML are delimited by double quotes.

```
ML> "this is a string";
    "this is a string" : string
```

The only nonprintable character permitted in a string is a blank. In particular the ASCII character for a new line is prohibited. Thus when a newline character is detected in a string, the cause is known to be a missing double quotes symbol, which prevents this sort of mistake from consuming more than one line of the input program before the mistake is reported. Nonprintable characters other than the blank can be inserted in a string via an escape sequence (these are described later).

The length of a string can be obtained using the built-in operator **size**.

```
ML> size "string";
    6 : int
```

The empty string has size zero.

```
ML> size "";
    0 : int
```

The ^ infix operator concatenates strings, as demonstrated in the next example.

```
ML> "abc" ^ "defg";
    "abcdefg" : string
```

There is no predefined substring operator in ML; however, it is easy to define one.

ML has no separate data type for characters. Characters can be considered strings of length one.

```
ML> "A"; "B";
    "A" : string
    "B" : string
```

All the 256 8-bit characters can be obtained using escape sequences.

Escape sequences.   Inside a string the backslash character has a special meaning other than the ASCII backslash character. It is the *escape character* in strings.   The ASCII characters without a common printable representation can put into string literals using escape sequences. The character ", which delimits string literals, and the backslash character itself can only be put into a string literal using escape sequences.

For example, the ASCII newline character is represented by \n and the tab character by \t. Both of these sequences represent a single character.

```
ML> size "A"; size "B"; size "\n"; size "\t";
    1 : int
    1 : int
    1 : int
    1 : int
```

The complete list of character sequences with special meanings is given in the following table:

sequence	meaning
\n	newline character
\t	tab
\\	\ (the ASCII backslash character)
\"	" (the ASCII double-quotes character)
\^*c*	control character
ddd	the 8-bit character
w···*w*\	formating

The character *c* can be any character in the continuous sequence of ASCII printable characters. All 256 8-bit characters can be obtained by the escape sequence *ddd*. The character *d* must be a decimal digit. So the legal escape sequences of this form are as follows:

\000 \001 \002 \003 ... \249 \250 \251 \252 \253 \254 \255

Note that **"\1234"** is a legal string of length two: **"}4"**, and **"\12A"** is *not* a legal string of length two. The sequence of characters *w*···*w* stands for any sequence of formating characters. The collection of formating characters must include the space, newline, tab, and formfeed characters. The sequence of characters *w*···*w*\ are ignored in any string. Escape sequences that do not fit any of the forms in the previous table are illegal and flagged by the system.

Here is a string with an embedded newline character:

```
ML> "... end of the first line\nthe beginning of the next ..."
    "... end of the first line\nthe beginning of the next ..." : string
```

Very long strings can be continued on the next line.

```
ML> "... extremely long string \
..> \extending across two lines ...";
    "... extremely long string extending across two lines ..." : string
```

This is the only way to break a string literal across a line.

The number of characters in a string that is actually printed out by the ML system can sometimes be controlled. (For instance, in SML of NJ this is controlled by the structure **System.Control.Print**.)

2.2.3 Boolean

The boolean values in ML have the names **true** and **false**. They are the only two members of the data type **bool**.

```
ML> true; false;
    true : bool
    false : bool
```

ML has the usual unary operation of negation

```
ML> not true;        (* negation *)
    false : bool
```

```
ML> not false;
    true : bool
```

Conjunction and disjunction are treated in ML as special cases of the conditional construct, so we defer their introduction until after the **if** expression.

There is the usual conditional expression in ML as in most languages. It is written as customary with the key words **if, then**, and **else**. The "else" part of the conditional is *not* optional; it must always be present. In addition, the type of the expression in the "else" part must be equal to the type of the expression in the "then" part. Here is an example.

```
ML> if true then "then" else "else";
    "then" : string
```

```
ML> if false then if true then 1 else 2 else if false then 3 else 4;
    4 : int
```

A key property of the **if** statement is that only the necessary branch is evaluated.

```
ML> if true then 2 else 37 div 0;
    2 : true
```

```
ML> if false then 37 div 0 else 3;
    3 : true
```

All the calculation in the other branch is spared, which is important when there is some sort of error or lengthy computation involved.

The operation of equality is important in connection with the data type of boolean values. This operation returns the boolean value **true** if its operands are identical, otherwise it returns **false**. Every basic data type (and every structured data type except functions) has its own infix equality operator.

```
ML> 1=1;
    true : bool
```

```
ML> 2=4;
   false : bool

ML> "string" = "string";
   true : bool
```

The test for equality is often used in an **if** expression.

```
ML> if 1=2 then 3 else 4;
   4 : int
```

An inequality operator **<>** is also built in. There are the other obvious built-in boolean operations: **<**, **>**, **>=**, and **<=**. These operators work for integers, real numbers, and strings.

There are two variants of the **if** statement that are provided in the ML language that have similarities with the binary boolean operations conjunction and disjunction. The issue is that, in the absence of side effects, there is no need to evaluate both arguments of these operations in all cases. For example, if x is false, then the value of x and y is false regardless of the value of y. This kind of evaluation is sometimes called *short-circuit evaluation* and is identical to special cases of the **if** statement in which one of the branches is a constant true or false. ML provides the operations **andalso** and **orelse** for short-circuit evaluation. These operations can be defined

$$x \text{ andalso } y = \text{if } x \text{ then } y \text{ else false}$$
$$x \text{ orelse } y = \text{if } x \text{ then true else } y$$

in terms of the **if** statement as indicated previously. All other special cases of the **if** statement can be obtained from these two operators using the **not** operator.

Other programming languages have short-circuit operations for the boolean connectives. In the programming language Ada there is **and then** and **or else** written as two words. In C these operations are written **&&** and **||**. The programming language Pascal does not have any built-in short-circuit operations. This was generally regarded as a defect. The usefulness of short-circuit evaluation can be seen by comparing the following two **if** statements. The first **if** statement contains an operator **&** that evaluates both its operands (such an operation is easily defined; see section 4.2.2).

```
if (not (n=0) & (37 div n = 4)) then ... else ...
if (not (n=0) andalso (37 div n = 4)) then ... else ...
```

If the integer n does happen to have the value zero, then the first **if** statement requires **37** to be divided by zero. Conversely, the second **if** statement takes the "else" branch without evaluating the second conjunct. The short-circuit operators do not commute, although the logical operations of conjunction and disjunction do. Interchanging the operands in the preceding **if** statement defeats the whole point.

```
if ((37 div n = 4) andalso not (n=0)) then ... else ...
```

The **if** statement rewritten this way does not prevent division by zero.

It is interesting to point out that the boolean data type can be defined in terms of other primitive features of the language. See section 5.1 on concrete data types.

2.2.4 Real

Real numbers are defined using the decimal point. The period separates the integer part from the fractional part.

```
ML> 3.14159;              (* an approximation of pi *)
    3.14159 : real
```

One or more digits must follow after the decimal point. The number can be written in "scientific notation" where the power of 10 is given after the exponent symbol **E**. (A lower case "e" is not accepted.)

```
ML> 123.456E7;
    1.23456E9 : real
```

The fraction part is optional if the exponent part is present. The set of real-number literals and the set of integer literals are disjoint; hence, the type of numeric literals can be determined from their form.

To summarize the three forms a real-number literal can take, we give the following regular expressions:

$$[\sim]dd^*.dd^* \qquad [\sim]dd^*\mathbf{E}[\sim]dd^* \qquad [\sim]dd^*.dd^*\mathbf{E}[\sim]dd^*$$

where d is any digit and $[\sim]$ means the minus sign is optional at that point. A real-number literal does not contain white space of any kind. A plus sign is not permitted before the exponent as in some languages. If the decimal point appears, then at least one digit must follow.

Some input is confusing, because it looks like a real-number literal. The character **E** immediately following a sequence of digits is not necessarily the exponent symbol. It is only when the following character is a digit or the minus sign. Here is some input that looks similar to the syntax of real number literals but is not. The right-hand side shows how the input is actually broken up into tokens by the scanner.

```
23EFG    = 23 EFG
23E 37   = 23 E 37
23E~AB   = 23 E ~ AB
23.4EFG  = 23.4 EFG
23.4E 37 = 23.4 E 37
23.4E~AB = 23.4 E ~ AB
A.0E~34  = A . 0 ~ 34
A.0E~BC  = A . 0 ~ BC
3.E~34   = 3 . ~ 34
3.ABC    = 3 . ABC
```

Most of this input is not legal in any context, because the period character can appear only in limited situations in the ML core language. In real numbers it can appear only between two digits. Other than inside a string, the period appears only in the token . . ., which appears in patterns for records. The period is used outside the core language in connection with modules.

Like the data type **int**, the operations of addition, subtraction, multiplication, and division are predefined for real numbers. For the first three operations the symbols are the same as the integer counterparts.

```
ML> 1.2 + 3.4;
    4.6 : real

ML> 1.2 - 3.4;
    ~2.2 : real

ML> 1.2 * 3.4;
    4.08 : real
```

The operation of dividing two real numbers is indicated by the identifier **/**.

```
ML> 7.2 / 4.8;
    1.5 : real
```

This operator is defined for real numbers only; the integer division function is named **div**.

The next examples introduce other predefined operations on real numbers.

```
ML> sqrt (2.0);                (*  square root       *)
    1.41421 : real

ML> ln (3.1415926535);         (*  natural logarithm *)
    1.14473 : real
```

The square-root function **sqrt** expects an argument of type **real** whose value is greater than or equal to zero. The natural logarithm function **ln** expects a real argument greater than zero. If an argument outside the domain of these functions is used, a run-time exception is raised. Exceptions are the subject of chapter 6.

The inverse of the **ln** is the exponential function.

```
ML> exp (3.1415926535);        (*  exponential function  *)
    23.1407 : real

ML> sin (3.1415926535 / 2.0);  (*  sine function     *)
    1.0 : real

ML> arctan (3.1415926535);     (*  inverse tangent  *)
    1.26263 : real
```

The trigonometric functions all work in units of radians.

Real numbers are currently implemented using the double precision floating-point arithmetic of the language C. Inevitably some precision is lost as seen in the next examples.

```
ML> 3.1415926535;
    3.141593 : real

ML> 2.7182818284;
    2.718282 : real
```

The operations on **real** numbers are plagued with the usual problems of arithmetic overflow, underflow, and so on.

2.2.5 Unit

The final basic data type in ML is the simplest. It is called **unit** because this data type has exactly one element. This one element is **()**, which we will call the *unit element*.

```
ML> ();
    () : unit
```

The opening and closing parentheses of the unit element must be adjacent. The unit element will not be recognized if there is any white space between the parentheses.

There are no operations on the element of the unit data type. What operations could there possibly be? It is reasonable to ask why there should be such a data type at all. In ML the unit data type is most often used with constructions that involve side effects, like assignment or input-output. This is much like the type **void** in ALGOL or ANSI standard C.

2.3 TUPLES, RECORDS, AND LISTS

There are several ways to build compound structures out of the elements of the basic types. In this section we look at three of these ways: tuples, records, and lists.

2.3.1 Tuples

A tuple is an ordered, heterogeneous collection of elements formed by separating the individual elements by commas and enclosing the whole structure in parentheses.

```
ML> (true, (), 1);
    (true, (), 1) : bool * unit * int

ML> (2, "ab", 2*2, 5.0);
    (2, "ab", 4, 5.0) : int * string * int * real
```

The type of a tuple is the cartesian product of the types of the elements. The "$*$" symbol is used as the cartesian product operator for data types as well as for multiplication. This overloading of the asterisk will never cause any confusion, because expressions and types are completely separate. It will always be clear from context whether an expression or a type is expected, and, hence, whether a product of numeric values or a cartesian product is wanted.

Tuples always consist of two or more elements. There are no tuples of one element. Parenthesizing a single value does not change it.

```
ML> ( 2 );
    2 : int
```

Here is a striking example.

```
ML> ((()));
    () : unit
```

The types of elements in a tuple are not limited to the five basic types but can be any types whatsoever. In particular tuples of tuples are possible, as in the next example.

```
ML> ((2,3,4), (true,3.3));
    ((2,3,4), (true,3.3)) : (int * int * int) * (bool * real)
```

The preceding tuple has five elements, but it is not a 5-tuple. It is a pair—a pair consisting of a triple and another pair. The difference is important; despite the natural mapping between the two structures, they are not interchangeable in ML.

It is natural now to expect the introduction of the projection functions to select elements from a tuple. Before we do so, we make two important points.

1. No functions are necessary to decompose structured data types. Pattern matching (see section 3.3) provides all the operations in an elegant and uniform manner for all types including user-defined types.
2. Tuples are a special form of records. Records will be discussed in the next section.

Here is an example demonstrating how to select the second component of a tuple.

```
ML> #2 ("one", 2, "three");
    2 : int
```

The other projection functions are denoted similarly. More about selection is included in the next section about records.

2.3.2 Records

Heterogeneous records with labeled fields are familiar data structures in languages like Pascal, Ada and C. ML has records too. A record literal is written with braces.

```
ML> {abscissa = 1.2, ordinate = 3.2};
    {abscissa = 1.2, ordinate = 3.2} : {abscissa: real, ordinate: real};
```

A record type is written with braces as well. The preceding record has one field labeled **abscissa** and another labeled **ordinate**. The type of both fields is **real**.

A key property of tuples is the order of the elements. In records the order of the fields makes no difference, because the fields are labeled. The following two records are equal even though the order of the fields has been switched.

```
ML> {abscissa = 1.2, ordinate = 3.2} = {ordinate = 3.2, abscissa = 1.2};
    true : bool
```

Of course, there is no limit to the number of fields in a record, or to their type. The following record has four fields of different types.

```
ML> {a = (), b = 2, c = ("s",2), d = 1};
    {a = (), b = 2, c = ("s",2), d = 1} :
      {a: unit, b: int, c: string * int, d: int}
```

Records can be nested within other records.

```
ML> {a = 2.3, b = {a="s", c=45}};
    {a = 2.3, b = {a="s", c=45}} : {a: real, b: {a: string, c: int}}
```

The "outer" record has fields named **a** and **b**. The "inner" record has fields named **a** and **c**. There is no problem with different records using the same field name. A single record, however, must give each field a different label.

It is possible to have a record with just one field, although this is not particularly useful.

```
ML> {one = (2.3, "string")};
    {one = (2.3, "string")} : {one: real * string}
```

Tuples are actually a special case of records with implicit label names. For example, the tuple **((),true,1)** is equivalent to the following:

```
ML> {1=(), 2=true, 3=1};
    ((), true, 1) : unit * bool * int

ML> {1=(), 3=1, 2=true};
    ((), true, 1) : unit * bool * int
```

Numeric labels can be used, even if the record is not a tuple. Here is an example.

```
ML> {1=(), 3=1};
    {1=(), 3=1} : {1:unit, 3:int}
```

Also mixing numeric and nonnumeric fields is permitted.

```
ML> {34564=1, b=2, b3=3, <*> =4};
    {34564=1, b=2, b3=3, <*> =4} : {34564:int, b:int, b3:int, <*>:int}
```

(The space after the nonnumeric label **<*>** is necessary as the equals sign is a legal constituent of a symbolic identifier.) Numeric fields must not begin with the digit **0**, however.

```
ML> {1=1, 01=01, 001=001}              (* Error! *)
Syntax error -- Numeric label may not begin with '0'.
(stdin), line =    1:
 {1=1, 01=01, 001=001};
........^
The token that caused the problem was: "01"
```

There is a primitive construct in the language for field selection. Although strictly speaking one is not necessary, it is convenient. The construct **#** *label*, where *label* is any numeric or nonnumeric label, can be used like a function to extract the indicated field from a record. So unlike most languages that use a special postfix form for field selection, ML provides an operator that is applied to a record. Here is an example.

```
ML> #a {a=3};
    3 : int

ML> # a{z=1.2, a=3, b=true, 4=()};
    3 : int

ML> #a (#b {b={a=3}});
    3 : int
```

Although the **let** construct has not been introduced yet, we cannot resist some whimsical examples of records.

```
ML> let val r = {1=3} in # r r end;
    3 : int
```

This example takes advantage of the fact that labels do not occupy the same name space as other identifiers.

```
ML> let val ### = 3 in # ## {## = ###} end;
    3 : int
```

This takes advantage of the fact that **##** is a legitimate (symbolic) identifier; hence, it is a legitimate label. Likewise **###** is a legitimate symbolic identifier. For the full story on the identifiers see section 3.1. Note that the spaces between **=** and symbolic identifiers are necessary.

2.3.3 Lists

Homogeneous lists of elements of any length can be built and manipulated in ML. In contrast tuples are heterogeneous and have fixed length. Lists are written using square brackets, and the individual elements are separated by commas. The empty list is written **[]**.

```
ML> [1,2,3,4];
    [1,2,3,4] : int list
```

```
ML> [(8,true),(5,false)];
    [(8,true),(5,false)] : (int * bool) list
```

Note that tuple elements and list elements are both separated by commas.

Two infix operators exist for augmenting lists. The concatenation operator, denoted by ::, adds an element to the front of a list. The append operator, denoted by @, joins two lists with the same type of elements.

```
ML> 1 :: [2,3,4]; 1 :: 2 :: [3,4];
    [1,2,3,4] : int list
    [1,2,3,4] : int list

ML> [1,2,3] @ [4,5];
    [1,2,3,4,5] : int list
```

All combinations of lists of tuples and tuples of lists are possible. Here are some complex examples.

```
ML> [("abcd", 4), ("xyz", 3)];
    [("abcd",4),("xyz",3)] : (string * int) list

ML> (["abcd", "xyz"], [4, 3]);
    (["abcd","xyz"],[4, 3]) : (string list) * (int list)

ML> [[2,4,6], [2,3,5,7], [2,4,8,16,32]];
    [[2,4,6],[2,3,5,7],[2,4,8,16,32]] : (int list) list
```

All lists can be represented by starting with the empty list and concatenating each element on individually. Thus **[1,2]** can be represented as **1::2::[]**. So with a symbol for the empty list and the concatenation operator all lists can be constructed. Hence, the empty list and :: are special operators known as constructors. The constructor for the empty list is named **nil**. The list constructors could be defined by the user and therefore, in principle, could be eliminated from the language. Because lists are so common in programming in ML, however, they are implemented as a primitive data structure.

Writing lists using square brackets is actually a notational convention. This convention is best understood as a translation T from the bracket notation to the unabbreviated form. The recursive definition of T is as follows:

$$T([]) = \text{nil}$$
$$T([x, y, \ldots, z]) = x :: T([y, \ldots, z])$$

For example, the translation of **[1,2]** is

$$1 :: \mathcal{T}([2]) = 1 :: 2 :: \mathcal{T}([]) = 1 :: 2 :: \text{nil}$$

This translation is important to remember when considering pattern matching on lists.

The same translation is important in the programming language PROLOG, because this translation explains how unification of lists is performed. In PROLOG the same abbreviation for lists is used as in ML, except that there is no special name for the empty list, it is written [].

The foregoing explains how lists are constructed. What about operations on lists? It might be expected that ML has primitive functions to take the first element off a list and also to return the rest of the list. Also, a function to distinguish empty lists from nonempty lists could be expected. These operations are not necessary, and can be defined, if desired, using pattern matching. The definition of the language standard does not require that these functions be present in the initial environment. However, SML of NJ docs provide them with the functions named **hd, tl** and **null**.

The definition of the language does require a function named **rev**, to reverse a list, and a function named **map**. The function **map** is the most important of several higher-order functions (see section 4.4) that manipulate lists. The use of lists often replaces the use of arrays in conventional languages. This makes them important in functional languages. Several unique techniques for manipulating lists, like the function **map** that applies a function to every element of a list, are needed to exploit the full potential of the data structures.

We have now covered most of the basic objects in the ML language with the exception of functions. Chapter 4 is devoted to the subject of functions.

2.4 ERROR MESSAGES

We have described the interaction with the ML system, and some of the simple objects and operations found in the ML language. Before we continue describing ML in more detail in the next chapters, it is appropriate to become familiar with the kind of error messages that will be encountered in running ML. The error messages provide useful clues as to the nature of the problem.

The error messages are divided up into five basic categories indicating the basic problem.

1. Syntax errors
2. Semantic errors
3. Semantic warnings
4. Type errors
5. Compiler errors

We examine each of the categories in turn to describe what happens when an error occurs. The total number of individual errors is quite large, and mostly self-explanatory, so we do not describe each one.

2.4.1 Syntax Errors

Syntax errors occur when input to the ML system cannot be recognized as any well-formed phrase of the language. Syntax errors print the file name and the line number where the error was detected. A caret (^) points to the token that caused the parser to report the error. Here is an example.

```
ML> 3 + rec;     (* Error! *)
Syntax error -- Expecting an expression.
(stdin), line = 45:
3 + rec;
......^
The token that caused the problem was "rec" (a keyword)
```

The error message usually indicates the last token parsed by the parser. If the token is an identifier, it mentions whether or not it is a keyword. This is useful in cases in which the programmer accidentally uses a keyword as an identifier.

Error recovery is for the most part quite primitive. If an error is detected, the remainder of the input line is thrown away.

2.4.2 Semantic Errors

Not all syntactically correct programs make sense. There are a few nonsyntactic rules that define the semantically correct ML programs. These rules will be discussed as they come up in later chapters. Violations of these rules make it impossible to interpret the program. All these errors are *fatal*, meaning the ML system cannot execute any code in response to the input.

The most common example of a semantic error is the case of an undefined variable. The ML system prints an error message indicating the problem.

```
Semantic error -- The identifier x is undefined.
```

Other semantic errors involve pattern matching.

2.4.3 Semantic Warnings

Some constructs are syntactically and semantically legal, but do not make much sense. In this case the compiler issues a *warning* in case the programmer made a mistake, but continues anyway under the assumption that the program might still be useful, perhaps in restricted cases.

These problems are infrequent and do not cause the ML system to give up on the program as in the case of fatal errors. The program is compiled and executed. Here is an example warning message.

```
Semantic warning -- Pattern in value binding not exhaustive.
```

The significance of these messages will be discussed as appropriate in later chapters.

2.4.4 Type Errors

Type errors occur in programs that do not manipulate data objects consistently. This is also a fatal error. A type error is detected when the ML system analyzes the input and before generating code to execute it.

Type errors do not print the line in which the inconsistency is found, since the input text is not kept after parsing. Here is a simple example of a type error.

```
ML> sqrt (2);                    (* Error! *)
Type error -- Cannot unify domain of function and its argument.
The function:  sqrt
Domain of fun: real
The argument:  2
Type of arg:   int
```

The square-root function works for real numbers only, not for integers—hence, the preceding type error.

The following is another example of a type error. This time the problem is that the branches of an **if** statement have different types.

```
ML> if true then 3 else 3.0;  (* Error! *)
Type error -- if statement type clash.
The "then" part has type:    int,
but the "else" part has type: real
The expression:  if true then 3 else 3.0
```

Type errors can be difficult to understand, because ML flags the first inconsistency that it finds. This inconsistency may not necessarily be the location of the error. Chapter 7 on types gives more details about how type checking works. This will contribute to understanding the errors produced when the ML system analyzes the types of expressions.

2.4.5 Compiler Errors

In rare cases, some ML programs exceed the capacity of the compiler. This can happen, for example, if a literal or identifier is more than eighty characters.

```
Compiler error -- Token buffer overflow.
```

Another compiler error is possible if the depth of nested procedures is too great. Different ML systems have different limitations. Some of these limits can be changed by regenerating the system. Of course, this may cause the executable version of the system to be larger.

There is one error in this category that cannot be solved in this way.

```
Compiler error -- Out of memory.
```

In this case the ML system was unable to obtain enough memory from the operating system to continue its own operation.

This error should not be confused with running out of memory during the execution of an ML program. This causes an exception to be raised at run time. Because the ML system performs garbage collection (reclaiming of memory no longer needed), only very large programs or very malicious programs should exhibit these problems.

■ Chapter 3

Value Bindings

There are many objects that can be manipulated by ML programs. We saw examples in the last chapter of integers and lists, to name two kinds. The data items manipulated by ML programs are commonly called *values*. The ability to give values a name, like a constant definition common in other programming languages, is essential for any serious programming. The act of bestowing a name on a value is called a binding of the name to a value. In this chapter we describe value bindings. In the first section we make clear just what the legal set of value identifiers is in ML. Then we can describe the various forms that value bindings have. Finally we describe pattern matching, a feature not found in many programming languages. Pattern matching expands the usefulness of value bindings by permitting bindings to occur according to the structure of values.

3.1 IDENTIFIERS

The ML objects introduced so far have been literals or predefined operations. The names of the operations **sin**, **+**, and so on are examples of a syntactic category in the language called identifiers. All identifiers are sequences of printable ASCII characters. Not all such strings are legal identifiers, however. The keywords like **if**, **val**, among others, are excluded. Apart from keywords we can say the usual sorts of strings beginning with a letter of the alphabet are identifiers in ML. In addition strings of symbols are also identifiers, so, for example, **+**, **–** and **<=>** are identifiers. They are ordinary identifiers that the ML programmer can use in value bindings at will. It just happens that **+** and **–**

are defined to have their customary meaning in the initial environment of the ML system.

The exact definition of identifiers is not crucial to the understanding of the ML language, so the next section can be skipped or skimmed.

3.1.1 Categories of Identifiers

Identifiers can be described according to their form or according to their use. Legal identifiers fall into one of three categories according to their form.

1. *Alphabetic*: This class of identifiers begins with a letter and continues with a letter, digit, underscore character, or apostrophe.
   The following are all examples of alphabetic identifiers:

   ```
   i A3 big_int SmallInt
   ```

2. *Prime*: This class of identifiers begins with the character ′ and continues with a letter, digit, underscore character, or apostrophe. Standard ML distinguishes special classes of prime identifiers: those beginning with ′′ are used for equality type variables, and those beginning with ′_ or ′′_ are used for imperative type variables (see section 7.5).

   The following are examples of prime identifiers:

   ```
   ′′_ ′1 ′a ′ab′′ ′′_c
   ```

   The following are not prime identifiers:

   ```
   ′! ′# a′
   ```

3. *Symbolic*: This class is composed of strings of the following characters:

   ```
   ! $ # % & * + - / : < = > ? @ \^ ` |~
   ```

   Some examples of this class of identifiers are as follows:

   ```
   <=> $$? * --
   ```

This is not quite the entire story of identifiers. Some sequences of characters are reserved because they are important to the syntax of the language. These sequences are called keywords or reserved words, and they cannot be used as identifiers. This is the entire list of reserved words for the core language:

```
abstype and andalso as case do datatype else end
exception fn fun handle if in infix infixr let local
 nonfix of op orelse raise rec then type val while
      ( ) [ ] {} , : ; ... | = => -> _ #
```

All the character strings in the three classes described previously are identifiers *except* for the reserved words. The string **then**, for example, is not an alphabetic identifier, because it is reserved for use in the syntax of the **if** construct. The string **=>** is not a symbolic identifier, because it is reserved for function definition. Some of the nonalphabetic keywords are single characters and serve as punctuation in the language. These characters, **() [] {} , ; .** cannot be a part of any identifier, whether alphabetic, prime, or symbolic.

Because symbolic and alphabetic identifiers are composed of disjoint sets of characters, they are recognized even if no white space separates them, as in the following examples:

$$x+y \ = x + y$$
$$A123!@B456 \ = A123 \ !@ B456$$

In all cases the longest possible identifier is recognized as the next token for the parser. This can be mildly counterintuitive in some unusual cases concerning symbolic identifiers. For example, assigning the contents of **x** to **y** is written **y:= !x** not **y:=!x**, which is interpreted to contain the identifier **:=!**. Another example is the unary minus symbol constrained by its type, which must be written **~ :int->int** not **~:int->int**. The last expression is interpreted as having the identifier **~:**.

We have just classified identifiers according to their form. Identifiers can also be classified according to their use in the following seven categories:

1. *Function symbols*: Names of values including constants like **nil** and **+**
2. *Constructors*: Special function symbols that construct elements of types
3. *Value variables*: Formal parameter names
4. *Type identifiers*: Names of types
5. *Type variables*: Place holders for types
6. *Exception identifiers*: Names of exceptions
7. *Label identifiers*: Field names for records

We conclude this section on identifiers by making a few general remarks.

- The same identifier can *simultaneously* have roles as an object and as a type. But exception and object names occupy the same name space.
- All literals are constructors even though they are not identifiers. This is important in pattern matching.

- The equals sign is both a keyword and a function symbol. In its role as a function symbol it cannot be rebound by the user to some other purpose. Hence, one can safely assume that it always means equality.
- The type identifiers **int**, **bool**, **string**, **list**, *****, and **->** can be rebound but only as ML values, not as type identifiers. Thus, the type of all literals in the language can be printed without a name conflict with user-defined types.

3.2 VALUE BINDINGS

Many languages, like Pascal and Ada, permit the declaration of a constant. Throughout the scope of the declaration the constant name has the value indicated by its declaration. The value of the constant cannot be changed (although the name might be used in another declaration). Typically, in these languages declaring constants is less frequent than declaring variables. In ML the reverse is true. The binding of a name to a value is one of the most common actions performed by the programmer. In ML the syntax for binding the identifier *id* to the value of the expression *exp* is: *id=exp*. Different kinds of bindings are possible. Value bindings are introduced by the keyword **val** to distinguish them from bindings of type identifiers (see chapter 5) and bindings of exception identifiers (see chapter 6). Thus a value binding has the form:

    val *id* = *exp*

There are simple, local, and multiple value bindings. In this section we discuss each sort of value binding in turn. Recursive bindings, which apply only to functions, are not discussed here. They are left to the chapter on functions.

3.2.1 Simple Value Bindings

A binding made in response to the ML prompt is called a *global binding*.

The scope of a global binding is the rest of the ML session. Here is an example.

```
ML> val a = 2;              (* Bind the value 2 to a.              *)
    val a = 2 : int
```

The identifier can now be used in the remainder of the session to refer to the value 2.

```
ML> a;                      (* Respond with the value of a.          *)
   2 : int
```

```
ML> 3*a + 4*a*a;            (* Use the value of a in an expression. *)
   22 : int
```

The value of any arbitrary expression can be bound to an identifier. The expression need not be in simplest form, as is **2** earlier. The expression is evaluated first, before being bound to the identifier.

```
ML> val b = 3 * 4 + 5;
   val b = 17 : int
```

A value bound in one binding can be used in another binding as well as expressions.

```
ML> val c = 2 * b;          (* Use value of b in binding of c.      *)
   val c = 34 : int
```

Having made one binding to the alphabetic identifier **a**, another global binding to the identifier **a** will hide the first binding. The other binding is still there (in the presence of functions it is possible to observe it), but it is no longer visible. The new binding has made a hole in its scope.

```
ML> val a = 3;              (* This binding hides previous bindings. *)
   val a = 3 : int
```

```
ML> a;                      (* Respond with value of visible binding. *)
   3 : int
```

Identifiers are not necessarily alphabetic, so for the sake of variety we give an expression bound to a symbolic identifier.

```
ML> val <=> = (~1,0,1);              (* A symbolic identifier <=> *)
   val <=> = (~1,0,1) : int * int * int
```

We have now discussed two distinct kinds of phrases in the language that are appropriate to enter to the ML system in response to the prompt for input. These phrases are expressions like **a+3** and declarations like **val b=a+3**. Actually the ML system is expecting a declaration when it prints the prompt for input. It treats an expression as a degenerate sort of declaration. When the user types in the expression **a+3** the system treats it exactly as if it had been the declaration **val it=a+3**. Every expression typed in to the system is implicitly bound to the identifier **it**. This is useful, if after typing an expression, the user then wants to refer to it in the next declaration. The use of **it** is illustrated in the following short dialog.

```
ML> 6*5*4;
    120 : int

ML> val c = it div (3*2);
    val c = 20 : int

ML> it;
    120 : int
```

3.2.2 Local Value Bindings

Global bindings, such as those in the previous section, have an effect for the remainder of the session. It is possible to localize the scope of a binding. This is done with the **local** and **let** constructs. We will look at the **let** construct first. The syntax of the **let** statement has the following form:

> **let val** id = exp_1 **in** exp_2 **end**

The scope of the binding of the identifier id to the value of the expression exp_1 is the expression exp_2. The **let** statement is an expression; its value is the value of exp_2, and its type is the same as the type of exp_2.

Here is an example of a global and a local binding.

```
ML> val a = 4;                    (* Global binding to a.    *)
    val a = 4 : int

ML> let val a = 5 in a+6 end;     (* Local binding to a.     *)
    11 : int
```

The local binding has no effect on the global bindings. If we ask for the value of **a** now, the old value is again visible.

```
ML> a;                            (* No change in a.         *)
    4 : int
```

Inside the expression **a+6** the binding **a** to **5** is current. Outside the **let** expression the binding **a** to **5** disappears and the previously current binding of **a** to **4** is again current.

It might be asked what good a local binding is. After all, if **a** is to have the value 5 in **a+6**, then the same effect is achieved by writing **5+6**. One good reason for a local binding is to improve the clarity of the programs. Consider the following example:

```
ML> let val p = 87187 * 37049 in (p, p+2, p+4) end;
    (3230191163, 3230191165, 3230191167) : int * int * int
```

The arithmetic progression of the integers in the preceding triple is apparent in its definition. It is important to note that a local binding can also save computational work. No matter how many times the variable is used in the body of expressions, its value is computed just once. In the preceding example, the value **p** will be computed once no matter how difficult a computation is required. Finally, the local binding plays a crucial role in polymorphism. More about this can be found in section 7.2.

Often the programmer wants to bind the value of the expression in the body of a **let** statement to some identifier. This can be done in the following manner:

```
ML> val pi2 = let val pi = 3.14 in 2.0 * pi end;
    val pi2 = 6.28 : real
```

There is a variant of the **let** construct, however, which is designed for this purpose. This construct is the **local** construct. The body of the **local** statement is another binding, not an expression. Here is the syntax.

$$\textbf{local val } id_1 = exp_1 \textbf{ in val } id_2 - exp_2 \textbf{ end}$$

The scope of the binding of id_1 to the value of exp_1 is between the **in** and the **end**, as is the case with the **let** expression.

Here is an example of the **local** declaration.

```
ML> local
..>    val pi = 3.14
..> in
..>    val pi2 = 2.0 * pi
..> end;
    val pi2 = 6.28 : real
```

This declaration has the same effect as the previous one. The binding to **pi2** extends beyond the **end** of the local construct. Only the binding to **pi** is local.

The following schema demonstrates the scope rules on nested **local** declarations.

```
(*  some initial bindings are visible before the declaration.    *)
local
  local
    val a = ...  (* initial bindings are visible here.          *)
  in
    val b = ...  (* initial bindings, and a are visible here.   *)
  end
```

```
in
  local
    val c = ...   (* initial bindings, and b are visible here.       *)
  in
    val d = ...   (* initial bindings, b and c are visible here.      *)
  end
end
(* the initial bindings and d are visible after the declaration.   *)
```

3.2.3 Multiple Value Bindings

The global bindings made in the previous paragraphs were made sequentially—one after another in the course of the dialog with the system. Bindings can be done simultaneously as well as sequentially. This is accomplished with a multiple value binding. A multiple value binding has any number of bindings separated by the keyword **and**.

```
ML> val a = 0 and b = 1 and c = 7.8;
    val a = 0 : int
    val b = 1 : int
    val c = 7.8 : real
```

Note the difference between the keyword **and**, which delimits the bindings in a multiple binding, and the keyword **andalso**, which is a boolean operation.

The bindings in the multiple binding construct are independent.

```
ML> let
..>   val c = 3 and d = 4     (* Two local, independent bindings.  *)
..> in
..>   (c * d) div 3
..> end;
    4 : int
```

No binding can use identifiers defined by bindings in the other branches. It would be incorrect to try to use this construct to form dependent bindings where the value of **d** depends on the value of **c**. The result is an unbound identifier. Of course, if **c** already had a binding in the outer environment, that binding would have been used. The result may not be what the programmer had intended.

```
ML> let val e = 5 and f = e+1 in e+f end;   (* Error! *)
Semantic error -- The identifier e is undefined.
```

The binding of the identifier **e** is not visible in the expression **e+1**. Unless a binding to **e** exists in the outer environment, the identifier **e** is undefined.

Often it is convenient to have a list of bindings in which each one requires the previous bindings. Such a sequential list of bindings is accomplished by listing them one after the other, just like the bindings at the top level.

```
ML> let
..>    val c = 3; val d = c+1;      (* These bindings are dependent *)
..> in
..>    (c * d) div 3
..> end;
    4 : int
```

(Actually the semicolons are not needed here, but we use them as a matter of style.) The same effect can be achieved by nested **let** constructs, although this approach is more verbose.

```
ML> let
..>    val c = 3
..> in
..>    let val d = c+1 in (c * d) div 3 end
..> end;
    4 : int
```

3.3 PATTERNS

Thus far in this chapter we have seen how to bind identifiers to objects. These objects can be any of the basic or structured objects described in chapter 2. It is now time to describe how a structured object can be decomposed into its constituent pieces. It might be expected that operators to destructure objects would be provided every time constructors are provided. Such an approach is certainly possible. In ML, however, decomposition is effected by pattern matching in the value-binding process. This elegant and general approach was first used in the programming language HOPE.

We begin by giving an example.

```
ML> val (fst, snd) = (4, 4.45);
    val fst = 4 : int
    val snd = 4.45 : real
```

The pair **(4, 4.5)** is evaluated. This value is matched against the pattern **(fst, snd)**. Then two bindings are performed: **4** to **fst** and **4.45** to **snd**.

The idea is that instead of binding an object to an identifier we generalize bindings to permit patterns. The object is destructured according to the pattern and the appropriate bindings are made. The general syntax for a value binding is thus

    val *pattern* = *expression*

A *pattern* is a term built primarily from identifiers and constructors. In the process of matching a pattern to a value, identifiers may match any value whatsoever and cause a binding to be made to the identifier. Constructors only match themselves and cause no binding to take place.

The simplest pattern consists of a single identifier. All the value bindings in previous sections used a simple identifier as the pattern in the syntax of a value binding. An identifier never fails to match a value, so thus far no discussion of pattern matching was necessary. Exactly one binding is caused by the execution of a value binding when the pattern is an identifier, namely the obvious binding of the value of the expression to the identifier.

The key to understanding patterns and their importance to ML is to understand what constructors are. This is discussed after we consider some simple examples of tuple patterns and record patterns.

3.3.1 Tuple and Record Patterns

The syntax for a tuple pattern is

    (*pattern*$_1$, ... , *pattern*$_n$)

where $n \geq 2$. The next example illustrates how a triple is decomposed using a pattern in a **val** binding.

```
ML> val (a,b,c) = (1,3,6);   (* Matching in declaration *)
    val a = 1 : int
    val b = 3 : int
    val c = 6 : int
```

As we have mentioned tuples are actually special cases of records. And so tuple patterns are special cases of record patterns. The previous example is the same as

```
ML> val {1=a, 2=b, 3=c} = {1=1,2=3,3=6};
    val a = 1 : int
    val b = 3 : int
    val c = 6 : int
```

Here are two examples of record patterns with nonnumerical field labels.

```
ML> val {abscissa=x, ordinate=y} = {abscissa=1.2, ordinate=3.2};
    val x = 1.2 : real
    val y = 3.2 : real

ML> val {abscissa=x, ordinate=y} = {ordinate=3.2, abscissa=1.2};
    val x = 1.2 : real
    val y = 3.2 : real
```

The order of the fields is immaterial as their label uniquely identifies the specific field.

In the context of records there is a special syntactic construct that enables a record pattern to ignore fields.

```
ML> val {b=x, ...} = {a=2, b="s", c=3.4, d=[1,2]};
    val x = "s" : string
```

This is especially useful because the programmer need not know the exact type of the value to be matched against a pattern with keyword "...," only that it contains certain fields. This works for tuples as well.

```
ML> val {2=x, ...} = (1,2,3);
    val x = 2 : int
```

The keyword "..." may only appear at the end of a record pattern.

3.3.2 Constructors

The binding of a value to an identifier as in

```
ML> val x = 3;
    val x = 3 : int
```

is a special case of matching a value to a pattern. In the case in which the pattern is simply an identifier, the matching always succeeds and exactly one binding takes place. In general a pattern with structure matches a value of the same structure and causes bindings of identifiers to subcomponents of the value. In effect the value is decomposed. Because this pattern matching works for values of all types, even user-defined types, there is no need for special operations for decomposition since the very operations (constructors) for constructing them are used in pattern matching to destructure them.

In this section we explain the role of constructors. We have already mentioned that **nil** and **::** are constructors. They are functions that construct lists. Constructors are similar to other functions, like addition, with respect to syntax. Like functions they can take arguments and be written in infix form. The construct **::** takes two arguments and constructs a list. Constructors are also represented by the same classes of identifiers like other functions. Constructors do not *do* anything, however; that is to say, they do not compute or modify any objects, they create them. In patterns, constructors act as indicators of an object's structure. Addition is not a constructor; it computes on integers. So **2+3** is not a pattern.

The constructor **nil** represents the empty list. Nonempty lists are constructed, and hence recognized by, the constructor **::**. For this purpose they are important in patterns. Here are some examples of patterns built using the constructors **nil** and **::**.

```
nil                   (* the empty list                  *)
x :: nil              (* a singleton list                *)
x :: y                (* a nonempty list                 *)
x :: y :: nil         (* a list with 2 elements          *)
x :: y :: z           (* a list with 2 or more elements *)
```

One can view the pattern as a tree with nodes labeled with a constructor. Recall that the constructor **::** is an infix operator and that it associates to the right. The last pattern written in prefix form is **::(x,::(y,nil))**. (Note that this is not a legal ML expression unless the infix status of **::** is revoked.)

The pattern **nil** matches the value **nil**, and no bindings are made. The pattern **nil** does not match **2::nil** or **2::1::nil**. The pattern **x::nil** does not match **nil**. It does match **2::nil**, and a binding of the value **2** to **x** is made. Here are some more examples.

Pattern	Matches	Bindings	Does not match
nil	nil	(none)	2::nil
x::nil	5::nil	x=5	nil or 2::1::nil
x::y	3::2::1::nil	x=3 and y=2::1::nil	nil
nil::x	nil::(1::nil)::nil	x=(1::nil)::nil	1::nil

We have seen that lists as expressions could be written using the bracket notation that stands for certain applications of the constructs **::** and **nil**. Some of these patterns, those that end with **nil**, can be written using the bracket notation and stand for exactly the same application of the list constructors as expressions. Here are those previous examples using the bracket notation.

Pattern	Matches	Bindings	Does not match
[]	[]	(none)	[2]
[x]	[5]	x=5	[] or [2,1]
x::y	[3,2,1]	x=3 and y=[2,1]	[]
[]::x	[]::[[1]]	x=[[1]]	[1]

We saw in the previous sections that tuples and records could be used in patterns. Is there some tupling operator that is a constructor? Tupling in ML has special syntax: a comma-separated list enclosed in parentheses; there is no special tupling identifier to serve as the constructor. The following table shows the bindings caused by pattern matching with tuple patterns.

Pattern	Matches	Bindings	Does not match
(x,y)	(1,2)	x=1 and y=2	(1,2,3)
(nil,x)	(nil,3.1)	x=3.1	(1,3.1)
(x,y,z::nil)	(1,2,3::nil)	x=1 and y=2 and z=3	(1,2,[3,2])
(1,x,(y,z))	(1,2,(3,4))	x=2 and y=3 and z=4	(1,2,3,4)

The most important constructors are those created by the programmer. This occurs when types are defined. See chapter 5.

3.3.3 Pitfalls of Pattern Matching

Along with the added flexibility of pattern matching with constructors come some possibilities that are subject to misunderstanding. One such problem concerns duplicate identifiers. In a pattern all the identifiers must be distinct.

```
ML> val (x,x) = (2,3);          (* Error!  *)
Semantic error -- The variable x is used more than once in pattern.
The pattern is (x,x)
```

The problem is the pattern **(x,x)**. This is not a legal ML pattern because all the variables must be distinct. This pattern is *not* interpreted, as it might be in the programming language PROLOG, as a tuple with equal components.

Patterns do not necessarily match all values. Some of these mismatches are caught by the type checker. For example,

```
ML> val (head::rest) = 3*4;     (* Error!  *)
Type error -- Cannot unify type of pattern with type of expression.
Pattern    head::rest
Exp        3*4
```

In this case the pattern was for a list, and the compiler determined that the type of the expression **3*4** is **int**. Even without matching the value against the pattern, which takes place at run time, the compiler knows that the match cannot possibly succeed. Even if the pattern and the expression do have the same type, the matching may fail at run time. This is illustrated in the next examples.

```
ML> val (head::rest) = [1,2,3] @ [4,5,6]
Semantic warning -- Pattern in value binding not exhaustive.
    head = 1 : int
    rest = [2,3,4,5,6] : int list
```

The problem here is that the pattern **head::rest** does not match all values
of type **int list**. The compiler can detect a problem but does not know the
run-time value that will be matched against the pattern. If the value matched
against the pattern was the empty list instead of the list **[1,2,3,4,5,6]** in
the preceding example, the binding is still type correct, but that matching fails.
This results in a run-time failure manifested by an exception **bind.**

```
ML> val (head::rest) = [] @ [];
UNCAUGHT EXCEPTION -- Bind
```

No binding takes place here, because the evaluation of the declaration is
interrupted. (Chapter 6 is about exceptions and exception handling.)

3.3.4 Wild-card Patterns

ML has several constructs to make pattern matching more convenient.
One is a special pattern that matches any expression. This wild-card pattern
is denoted by the underscore character. Here it is used to discard the second
member of a triple, and in the next example it is used to discard the second
and fourth member of a 4-tuple.

```
ML> val (x,_,y) = (1,2,3);
    val x = 1 : int
    val y = 3 : int

ML> val (x,_,y,_) = (1,2,3,4);
    val x = 1 : int
    val y = 3 : int
```

The wild-card pattern is like an anonymous identifier that matches any value,
but does not cause a binding to take place. This permits a pattern to ignore
some part of the structure of the value.
Here is another example of the wild-card pattern using lists.

```
ML> val head :: _ = [1, 2, 3];
Semantic warning -- Pattern in value binding not exhaustive.
    val head = 1 : int
```

In this example, the remainder of the list is discarded, and only the first element of the list is bound to an identifier. The pattern does not match the empty list, so the compiler issues a warning.

3.3.5 Layered Patterns

Sometimes it is convenient to have a name for a value as well as names for the subcomponents. The patterns thus far presented permit an object to be destructured into its subcomponents, but there is no way to refer to the whole without creating it again from the pieces. Consider the pattern consisting of the single variable **x**. In a value binding this pattern binds the name **x** to the whole object. In contrast, the pattern **(fst, snd)** binds the names **fst** and **snd** to the two subcomponents of a pair. What if the programmer wants the name **x** to refer to the whole structure *and* **fst** and **snd** to refer to the subcomponents? The inconvenience is ameliorated by introducing a new kind of pattern. This pattern does not correspond to any new form of structure or object in ML; it represents a means by which more names can be bound to objects and their subcomponents. The syntax for the layered pattern is

identifier **as** *pattern*

We illustrate the use of a layered pattern on a pair as described earlier.

```
ML> val x as (fst,snd) = (2, true);
    val x = (2, true) : int * bool
    val fst = 2 : int
    val snd = true : bool
```

Three bindings are made.

The following is an example that also causes three bindings to occur. The entire list is bound to the identifier **list**, the head of the list is bound to **head**, and the tail of the list is bound to **tail**.

```
ML> val list as head :: tail = [1, 2, 3];
Semantic warning -- Pattern in value binding not exhaustive.
    val list = [1, 2, 3] : int list
    val head = 1 : int
    val tail = [2, 3] : int list
```

3.3.6 Literals

All the literals are patterns, too; they match values equal to themselves. Literals used as patterns do not cause any bindings to occur. For example, the literal **1** matches the value **1**.

```
ML> val (x,1) = (7,1);
Semantic warning -- Pattern in value binding not exhaustive.
   val x = 7;
```

The pattern **(x,1)** does not match all pairs, for example, it does not match **(7,2)**. Hence, the warning by the ML system.

```
ML> val 1 = 1;
Semantic warning -- Pattern in value binding not exhaustive.
Semantic warning -- No identifiers declared in pattern.
The pattern:  1
   (no bindings)
```

This value binding is quite pointless but legal. The ML system warned that no binding would occur and responded to the declaration by printing **(no bindings)**. Literals as patterns are occasionally useful in connection with more complex patterns. There is no point in excluding them from patterns as they are harmless.

   If the value does not match the pattern, an exception is raised at run time.

```
ML> val 1 = 2;
Semantic warning -- Pattern in value binding not exhaustive.
Semantic warning -- No identifiers declared in pattern.
The pattern:  1
UNCAUGHT EXCEPTION -- Bind
```

   Of course, literals of other types **bool**, **string**, and **real** are legal patterns. Negative literals of type **int** and **real** are permitted. Recall that no white space separates the negation symbol from the rest of the negative literal. If there is white space after the negation symbol, then the symbol ~ is the unary negation function. This function is not a constructor, so **~ 2** is not a legal pattern. But **~2** is.

   Not all decimal numbers can be represented exactly using a binary system. Most implementations of the real numbers will be binary. So testing for equality is subject to the vagaries of machine arithmetic. Hence, patterns of type **real** should be used with care.

3.3.7 Syntax of Patterns

We summarize the discussion on patterns by giving the syntax of patterns.

$$<pattern> ::= <identifier>$$
$$<pattern> ::= <constructor>$$
$$<pattern> ::= <constructor> (<pattern>_1, \ldots, <pattern>_n)$$
$$<pattern> ::= \_$$

$<pattern> ::= (<pattern>_1, \ldots, <pattern>_n)$

$<pattern> ::= <identifier>$ **as** $<pattern>$

$<pattern> ::= \{<label>_1 = <pattern>_1, \ldots, <label>_n = <pattern>_n\}$

$<pattern> ::= \{<label>_1 = <pattern>_1, \ldots, <label>_n = <pattern>_n, \ldots\}$

The last rule for patterns uses the keyword **. . .** to match the rest of a record. This should not be confused with the use of **. . .** to indicate that a record pattern contains any number of fields explicitly given by the programmer and separated by commas. Also note that binary constructors, if so declared, can be written in infix form; this is not reflected in the syntax given earlier.

■ Chapter 4

Functions

ML is a functional programming language. Not surprisingly, function objects are the most important values in an ML program, and for this reason the present chapter is devoted entirely to them. Function objects are values that have status equal to other values, like integers, tuples, and lists. In particular, operations can take functions as arguments and can return functions. This is quite different from conventional programming languages, which discriminate against functions, because the implementation of functions does not fit the traditional stack-based model.

The usual control constructs found in a conventional, imperative language such as **for** and **while** loops, are less important in a functional language, because most of the computation is not done on modifiable or mutable values. Functions and recursion provide a different and elegant means to write programs by continually building new pieces of the solution from old pieces of the input.

4.1 DEFINITION OF FUNCTIONS

Functional languages like ML have their theoretical origins with Church's lambda calculus. In the lambda calculus, the function with formal argument x and body b is written $(\lambda x.b)$. In ML this is rendered using the keywords **fn** and **=>** as **(fn x=>b)**. (The parentheses are not necessary.) The body of the function b is any ML expression. The body probably contains the identifier x in it, as otherwise the function would be constant. Here is an example.

```
ML> (fn x => x+1);        (* A function object: successor function *)
```

```
[function] : int -> int
```

Notice that there is no printable representation of a function value in ML. There is no point in keeping a textual representation of the function around, becasue it is likely to be large, and there is no point in printing an internal representation of the function that will not be meaningful to the programmer. So the ML system prints **[function]** for the value of any function.

Functions can be bound to variables at the top level using the **val** construct just as any other value:

```
ML> val f = (fn x => x+1);   (* Bind f to the successor function   *)
    val f = [function] : int -> int
```

Having defined a function object and bound it to **f**, we can ask ML to print the value of **f**.

```
ML> f;
    [function] : int -> int
```

Its value is the function object itself, which, as we have remarked, does not have a printable representation. More interestingly, we can apply the function object **f** to actual arguments.

```
ML> f (2);               (*  Function application            *)
    3 : int

ML> f 2;                 (*  Parens not needed, if arg a token.  *)
    3 : int
```

Function application is denoted by the juxtaposition of the function and its argument. It is an invisible infix operator. The syntax of function application is simply: exp_1 exp_2. The first expression must evaluate to a function. The second expression is the actual argument passed to the function.

The expression that is applied to another expression must be a function. That is to say, the type of the expression must be <type>-><type>. If it is not, then a type error occurs.

```
ML> 3 2;             (*  Error!  *)
Type error -- Expression in function position is not a function.
The expression is  3
Its type is        int
```

Not only must the expression be a function, but its domain must also match the type of the argument. If it is not, then ML reports a type error. The function

f defined earlier has type **int->int** and should not be applied to something not of type **int**.

```
ML> f (true);        (* Error!  *)
Type error -- Domain of function does not match argument.
The function is f
Its domain is    int
The argument is true
Its type is      bool
```

It is important to note that ML catches type errors when it statically analyzes the expression, not when it runs them.

As an operator, application binds more tightly than any other operator. For example, the following expression yields the value 12 and not 9.

```
ML> f 2 * 4;
    12 : int
```

Hence, it might be clearer to write **(f 2)*4**. Parentheses can be inserted anywhere in an ML expression. Furthermore, application is left associative. That means that **f g a** is equivalent to **(f g) a**, or, in words, **f** applied to **g** and the result applied to **a**.

Below is another expression. This time two function definitions are involved.

```
ML> #1 (fn x => x+1, fn y => y-1) 8;
    9 : int
```

We have the predefined function **#1** applied to a pair, and the result applied to **8**. Thus **#1** selects the first function, the successor function, and that function applied to **8** yields the answer **9**.

We have seen one way to define a function in ML: by binding a functional expression to an identifier, as in **val f=(fn *x*=>b)**. This way of defining a function is given an alternative syntax in keeping with the customary way of writing definitions: **fun f(*x*)=b**. Here is a simple function definition written in two different, but equivalent, ways.

```
ML> val f = (fn n => n+1); (* Definition of the function f.       *)
    val f = [function] : int -> int

ML> fun f (n) = n+1;        (* Same function, alternative syntax. *)
    val f = [function] : int -> int
```

This alternative syntax for function bindings using the keyword **fun** is clearer and less verbose, so we use it almost exclusively. We will use the keyword

fn only to define anonymous functions. Such functions are usually used in some auxiliary capacity and do not require a name. We will discuss function bindings using the keyword **fun** in more detail later.

Functions can take arguments of any type whatsoever and return values of any type. The function **h** below returns tuples. The function **j** returns integer lists.

```
ML> fun f(x) = x+2; fun g(x) = x*3;   (* h and j use these functions. *)
    val f = [function] : int -> int
    val g = [function] : int -> int

ML> fun h (x) = (f x, g x);  h (4);  h (7);
    val h = [function] : int -> (int * int)
    (6,12) : int * int
    (9,21) : int * int

ML> fun j (x) = [f x, g x];  j (4);  j (7);
    val j = [function] : int -> (int list)
    [6,12] : int list
    [9,21] : int list
```

4.1.1 Resolving Free Identifiers

With the introduction of functions it is no longer obvious which binding to an identifier is the one that governs the value of the identifier. Previously, when all bindings were at the top level, the most recent binding was the governing binding. Now with functions we may have identifiers (other than the formal arguments) in the function bodies. The binding that determines the value of the identifier could be obtained relative to the function call or relative to the function definition.

In the example below we define a function **f** using an identifier **a**, which is not a formal parameter. The value for **a** is obtained from a previous binding to **a** at the top level.

```
ML> val a = 1;
    val a = 1 : int

ML> fun f(x) = x+a;   f(4);
    val f = [function] : int -> int
    5 : int
```

What happens to the function **f** when this binding is eclipsed by another binding to **a** with a different value?

```
ML> val a = 3;
    val a = 3 : int
```

```
ML> f(4);                    (* f(4) still has the value 5. *)
    5 : int
```

Nothing happens! The function definition still depends on the first binding of the identifier **a** and is in no way affected by any subsequent bindings.

This entire example can be wrapped up in one expression as follows:

```
ML> let val a = 1 in
..>    let fun f(x) = x+a in
..>       let val a = 3 in
..>          f(4)
..>       end
..>    end
..> end;
    5 : int
```

The environment in which the function **f** is defined, namely the one in which **a** is bound to 1, is the environment that governs the value of **a** when the function **f** is executed. This holds even if the environment in which **f** is called, namely the one in which **a** is bound to 3, is different. This is called *lexical scoping* or *static binding*, because the environment can be determined from the lexical structure of the program. Notice that lexical scoping is different from the approach that chooses the most recent, active binding (this is called *dynamic binding*). The most recent binding to the identifier **a** in the execution of the preceding program is to **3**.

4.1.2 Recursive Functions

Recursive function definitions are allowed in ML. Throughout the body of the function the name of the function refers to the function being defined. For example, the obvious definition of the factorial function works as expected.

```
ML> fun fact (n) = if n=0 then 1 else n*fact(n-1);
    val fact = [function] : int -> int

ML> fact (15);
    1307674368000 : int
```

But the following definition for **fact** fails.

```
ML> val fact = (fn n => if n=0 then 1 else n*fact(n-1));
Semantic error -- The identifier fact is undefined.
```

The problem is that the scope of value bindings do not begin until after the end of the declaration. In this case the use of the identifier **fact** is not legal until after the declaration. This makes the definition of recursive functions impossible. So ML permits recursive value bindings, indicated by the keyword **rec**, for values that are functions.

```
ML> val rec fact = (fn n => if n=0 then 1 else n*fact(n-1));
    val fact = [function] : int -> int
```

We did not mention **rec** bindings in the previous chapter on value bindings as they pertain only to functions. Function bindings with the keyword **fun** are actually a derived construct and can be totally replaced using **rec** value bindings (see section 4.5).

Mutually recursive definitions are made using the **and** construct as the next example demonstrates. We define two recursive functions simultaneously: one to determine if a number is odd, and another to determine if a number is even. Of course, we could use the predefined function **mod** but choose to define each one in terms of the other.

```
ML> fun Odd (n) =
..>    if n=0 then false else Even (n-1)
..> and Even (n) =
..>    if n=0 then true else Odd (n-1);
    val Odd = [function] : int -> bool
    val Even = [function] : int -> bool
```

It would not be possible to define **Odd** first and then **Even**, as **Even** would be undefined in the definition of **Odd**. Likewise **Even** could not be defined first. Simultaneous and recursive bindings are indispensable in defining mutually recursive functions.

4.2 PARAMETER CORRESPONDENCE

Thus far all the examples of functions have had just one argument. In fact, all functions in ML are unary—that is, they expect exactly one argument. The argument can be a tuple, of course. So nothing is sacrificed to obtain this extreme conceptual elegance. Nevertheless, the programmer will initially be disappointed that functions cannot have more than one argument. We will see how the pattern-matching mechanism of ML will fully restore the convenience of functions with more than one argument (plus add a great deal more). Suppose we want to write a function **f** that divides the elements of two integers. Because functions must have one argument, we write the following:

```
ML> fun f(x) = (#1 x) div (#2 x);
    val f = [function] : (int * int) -> int
```

where the functions **#1** and **#2** extract the first and second elements from a pair. Now consider the following dialog.

```
ML> val p = (12,3);    (* define a pair p                    *)
    val p = (12,3) : int * int

ML> f (p);             (* function f applied to pair p       *)
    4 : int

ML> f (12,3);          (* function f applied to pair (12,3)  *)
    4 : int
```

This last expression is suggestive. It is parsed as one ML expression juxtaposed with another expression. This is unambiguously recognized as function application. It would be convenient if a similar construction worked for function definition. In fact, it does. Thus far we have used only a single variable as the formal parameter name in function definitions. Many programming languages permit a more general kind of association between formals and actuals. Most often a list of formals is permitted that must match a list of the same length of actuals. ML generalizes this notion of a parameter list to the notion of a pattern. We already discussed patterns in section 3.3 in connection with value bindings, and the same binding mechanism described there is used with functions.

For example, we can define the function **f** that divides two integers as follows:

```
ML> fun f (x,y) = x div y;
    val f = [function] : (int * int) -> int
```

The meaning of this definition is intuitively clear from experience with mathematical notation or other programming languages, without even knowing about patterns. The actual argument to the function **f** is to be matched against the pattern **(x,y)**. As a consequence **x** is bound to the first element of the actual argument, and **y** is bound to the second element. Notice that we are guaranteed that the actual argument is a pair, since the pattern **(x,y)** requires the type of the argument to be a pair. The ML system of types ensures that **f** is only applied to pairs. The following function **g** expects a triple for its argument:

```
ML> fun g (x,y,z) = x+2*y*z;
    val g = [function] : (int * int * int) -> int
```

The function **h** has a pair as its argument and its return value.

```
ML> fun h (x,y) = (x div y, x mod y);
    val h = [function] : (int * int) -> (int * int)
```

The following is an example of a more substantive function.

```
ML> fun roots (a,b,c) =
..>    let
..>      val d = sqrt (b*b - 4.0*a*c)
..>    in
..>      ((~b + d) / (2.0*a), (~b - d) / (2.0*a))
..>    end;
    val roots = [function] : (real * real * real) -> (real * real)
```

It returns a pair of real numbers corresponding to the real roots of the equation $ax^2 + bx + c = 0$. If the quantity **b*b-4.0*a*c** is negative, then a run-time exception is raised (see chapter 6).

The use of patterns in the previous examples is just like the positional correspondence of parameters in most programming languages. This is just the beginning, however. Other patterns can be used, for example, layered patterns. With layered patterns it is possible to bind formal parameters to input structures and their substructures simultaneously.

```
ML> fun h (x as (fst,snd)) = (x, fst div snd);
    val h = [function] : (int * int) -> ((int * int) * int)
```

Tuples of tuples are also possible.

```
ML> fun h ( (x,y), (a,b,c) ) = f(x,y) - g(a,b,c);
    val h = [function] : ((int * int) * (int * int * int)) -> int
```

The formal argument of the function **h** is a pair consisting of a pair and a triple. When the substructure of an object is unimportant, it can be ignored by taking advantage of the fact that functions always have one argument no matter how complex the pattern is in the definition. For example, the function **g** defined earlier expects a triple for its argument as is immediately apparent from its definition. Also **f** expects a pair. These data structures are not important in the definition of the function **h**, which merely passes the arguments to **f** and **g** without examining them. We can also define the function **h** as follows:

```
ML> fun h (x,y) = f(x) - g(y);
    val h = [function] : ((int * int) * (int * int * int)) -> int
```

The patterns used in the definitions of **f** and **g** make no difference in how these functions are called in **h**.

4.2.1 Defining Functions by Case Analysis

Allowing the formal arguments of function to be associated by pattern matching to the actual arguments raises the question about different definitions for different patterns. In fact, such a general mechanism is provided for in ML. For example, the function to sum the elements of an integer list can be defined by cases. In one case the argument is the empty list, in the other case a nonempty list.

```
ML> fun sum (nil) = 0 | sum (head::tail) = head+sum(tail);
    val sum = [function]
```

The general syntax of a function object is:

$$\text{fn } pat_1 \Rightarrow exp_1 \mid \ldots \mid pat_n \Rightarrow exp_n$$

The argument to the function is matched against the patterns until the matching succeeds. This may cause some bindings to occur. These bindings can be used in the evaluation of the appropriate expression.

All the patterns must match values of the same type. For example,

```
ML> fun
..>  f (x,y)   = x+y+1    |
..>  f (x,y,z) = x+y+z+2  |
..>  f _       = 3        ;
Type error -- Patterns of rule sequence don't have same type.
Expecting type:  int * int
But pattern:     (x, y, z)
has type:        'a * 'b * 'c
```

is not legal. The first pattern matches a pair, and the second matches a triple. The type of the function **f** is ambiguous. Such a function definition is not type correct. (Notice that the polymorphic type **'a->int** is not an option. The structure of the input argument is important, and it would have to be known at run time to implement the function **f** as having type **'a->int**.)

When binding a function object to an identifier, the **fun** binding form

$$\text{fun } id \ pat_1 \Rightarrow exp_1 \mid \ldots \mid id \ pat_n \Rightarrow exp_n$$

is equivalent to

$$\text{val rec } id = \text{fn } pat_1 \Rightarrow exp_1 \mid \ldots \mid pat_n \Rightarrow exp_n$$

Explicit use of the pattern matching can be obtained using the case statement. The syntax for the **case** construct in ML is as follows:

```
case exp of pat₁ => exp₁ | ... | patₙ => expₙ
```

The preceding function **sum** can be defined using the case statement.

```
fun sum(x) =
 case x of
  nil        => 0             |
  head::tail => head + sum(tail);
```

Using the **case** statement generally requires more space, so we favor the other
style of function definition. Actually, defining functions by case analysis can
be explained in terms of the **case** statement (see section 4.5).

All the patterns discussed in connection with value bindings in section 3.3
can be used in function definitions (and in the case statement). The wild-card
pattern used in conjunction with other patterns in an analysis by cases means
"else" or "otherwise." This is an example.

```
ML> fun f(0) = "zero" | f(_) = "nonzero";
   val f = [function] : int -> string
```

The order of patterns does make a difference.

```
ML> fun f(_) = "nonzero" |
..>     f(0) = "zero";
Semantic warning -- Redundant patterns in match.
    _ => ...
--> 0 => ...
   val f = [function] : int -> string
```

This function always returns the string **"nonzero"** regardless of its argument.
The ML system issues a warning if a pattern is unnecessary and, hence, never
executed.

Parameter association using patterns is subject to the same errors as value
binding. In particular, patterns with a variable occurring more than once are
not legal in function definitions any more than in value bindings.

It is possible to have a pattern that does not exhaust all the possibilities.
Even several patterns may not. For example, the pattern **head::rest** does
not match all lists. It matches nonempty lists, but it does not match the list
nil. The pattern might be used in the definition of a function, like in the
subsequent function **h.**

```
ML> fun h (head::rest) = head+1;
Semantic warning -- Patterns not exhaustive in def'n of function h.
   val h = [function] : (int list) -> int
```

```
ML> h (nil);
UNCAUGHT EXCEPTION -- Match
```

Applying the function **h** to the empty list causes a run time exception to be raised. This will only happen to functions which have been flagged by the compiler as containing patterns that are not exhaustive. Such an event can happen even to tuples.

```
ML> fun f (x,y,2) = x+y+2;
Semantic warning -- Patterns not exhaustive in def'n of function f.
   val f = [function] : int * int * int -> int

ML> f (1,2,3);
UNCAUGHT EXCEPTION -- Match
```

Here is an example of a function with a list as the domain.

```
ML> fun f[x,y,z] = (x,x+y+1,x+y+z+2);
Semantic warning -- Patterns not exhaustive in def'n of function f.
   val f = [function] : int list -> (int * int * int)

ML> f [1,2,3];
   1,4,8 : int * int * int

ML> f [1,2];
UNCAUGHT EXCEPTION -- Match
```

When **f** is applied to lists with lengths other than **3**, the exception **Match** is raised.

4.2.2 Parameter Passing

All parameters are evaluated before the body of the function is executed. This method of parameter passing is known as *call by value*.

It is impossible to write a function to act as an **if** statement in ML, because arguments are evaluated before the call. One might try the following **If** function:

```
ML> fun If (x,y,z) =
..>   if x then y else z;
```

There is a context in which this **If** function differs from the ML **if** statement. On the call **If(true,0,4 div 0)** the division by zero is not avoided as it would be in an ML **if** statement, because all arguments to the function **If** are evaluated before the function is executed.

This partial evaluation is the special property of the **if** statement and the **andalso** and **orelse** constructs which requires that they be part of the language. The programmer cannot obtain this behavior using functions that pass their arguments by value. However, it is possible to write boolean operators that evaluate both their arguments and even give them the customary infix syntax.

```
ML> infix 6 or;
    symbol "or" given infix status (left assoc, precedence=6).

ML> fun x or y = x orelse y;
    or = [function] : bool * bool -> bool

ML> infix 7 &;
    symbol "&" given infix status (left assoc, precedence=7).

ML> fun x & y = x andalso y;   (* & is a symbolic identifier *)
    & = [function] : bool * bool -> bool
```

The **infix** directive tells the parser that the symbol is binary and that it is used between its two arguments. The precedence of the symbol must be given in relation to the other infix symbols known to the parser. The higher the precedence the more tightly the operator binds. Symbols are given left associativity unless the directive **infixr** is given. Among different symbols of the same precedence it is best to parenthesize the expressions appropriately. Note that the infix status of a symbol does not follow scope rules and can only be issued at the top level.

4.3 POLYMORPHISM

There is no restriction on the type of the range or on the type of the domain of a function. We have seen that if the domain of a function is a tuple, we can think of it as a function of more than one argument. We have seen examples of functions from lists to tuples, and many other types. Functions can also have functions as arguments and return them as values. This is extremely valuable especially in conjunction with polymorphism, and we will examine such functions after we discuss polymorphism.

As long as a function does not make use of the specific structure of its argument the function will work on arguments with arbitrary structure. For example, the identity function **(fn x=>x)** ought to work for values of type **int, real, string,** or any type whatsoever. A function is said to be *polymorphic* when it works for elements of more than one type. The ML system permits polymorphic functions whenever possible, and however much is possible. This means that if a function requires a list, a tuple, or a record, say, but otherwise does not take advantage of the specific structure of the subcomponents, then the types of the subcomponents are not constrained in any way. For example, the functions to take the first and second of any pair work for all pairs, regardless of the types of the elements of the pair.

```
ML> fun fst (x,y) = x;
    val fst = [function] : ('a * 'b) -> 'a

ML> fun snd (x,y) = y;
    val snd = [function] : ('a * 'b) -> 'b
```

The types of these functions contain type variables **'a** and **'b** indicating that any type can be substituted in their place. All type variables begin with an apostrophe; hence, they are distinct from all other identifiers. All the types we have encountered thus far have not contained any type variables. These types are called *monomorphic*. Types with type variables are called *polymorphic* or *polytypes*. An *instance* of a polymorphic type is a type created by substituting a type for a type variable. For example, the following types are instances of **('a*'b)->'a** (the type of **fst**):

```
    (int * int) -> int
    ((bool list) * string) -> (bool list)
    (int * 'b) -> int
    (('c list) * 'b) -> ('c list)
```

The function **fst** can assume all these types when necessary; hence, it is a polymorphic function. The next two examples show **fst** applied to elements of different types.

```
ML> fst (2,3);
    2 : int

ML> fst ([true, false], "string");
    [true, false] : bool list
```

There are a couple of things to notice about polymorphic types. First, the names of the type variables do not matter, just as the names of formal parameters do not matter in function definitions. Second, a type variable denotes the same type throughout the entire type expression. When we substituted **('c list)** for **'a** above, we had to substitute **('c list)** everywhere **'a** appeared.

Some of the functions we have already encountered are polymorphic. In particular the predefined functions manipulating lists are polymorphic, as their usefulness depends on manipulating lists of any type.

```
nil  : 'a list
::   : ('a * 'a list) -> 'a list
@    : ('a list * 'a list) -> 'a list
```

Here are some examples.

```
ML> nil @ nil;
    nil : 'a list

ML> 3 :: nil;
    [3] : int list

ML  nil :: nil;
    [nil] : ('a list) list
```

Of course, the programmer will want to define polymorphic functions. This does not require any additional constructs (like **generic** in Ada) or any extra thought whatsoever. If a function definition does not constrain the structure of the data, then the ML system will automatically note that the function could be used on different types of data. For example, the function that switches a pair of values does not care what the structure of the first element of the pair is, nor what the structure of the second element is, only that the input is a pair.

```
ML> fun switch (x,y) = (y,x);
    val switch = [function] : ('a * 'b) -> ('b * 'a)
```

This, the obvious, definition does not require **x** and **y** to have any particular structure. The definition does not use **x** and **y** as a list, a function, a record, or anything. Hence, the ML system concludes that the type of **x** can be anything **'a** and the type of **y** can be anything **'b**. It does conclude the input must be pair (**'a,'b**), that the output must be a pair (**'b,'a**), that the type of the first element of the input pair is the same type as the second element of the output pair, and that the type of the second element of the input pair is the same type as the first element of the output pair. Thus, the function **switch** can be used on pairs of different types of elements, similar elements, complex elements, or simple elements.

```
ML> switch (2, "abc");
    ("abc",2) : string * int

ML> switch (2,3);
    (3,2) : int * int

ML> switch ([], (fn x =>x) );
    ([function], nil) : ('a -> 'a) * ('b list)
```

The function **null**, although likely predefined, is a polymorphic function of lists that is quite easily defined by the programmer.

```
ML> fun null (nil) = true | null (_::_) = false;
    val null = [function] : 'a list -> bool
```

The length function is another simple example.

```
ML> fun length (x) =
..>    if null x then 0 else length (tl x) + 1;
    val length = [function] : 'a list -> int
```

The length function requires **x** to be a list but does not require the elements of the list to be any particular type. Hence, the type of the domain is **'a list**.

4.4 HIGHER-ORDER FUNCTIONS

Functions can have arguments of any kind and can return values of any kind. In particular, functions can take other functions as arguments and can return other functions. Such functions are called *higher order*. Higher-order functions are quite common in ML and, in fact, quite useful. These functions permit elegant solutions to problems that are obscure when solved by programs in conventional programming languages.

4.4.1 Functions as Arguments

We said functions can be used as arguments to other functions. Here are some simple examples using the higher-order function **apply3**.

```
ML> fun apply3 (f) = f(3);
    val apply3 = [function] : (int -> 'a)  -> 'a
```

This function applies its argument (which is also a function) to the value 3. Here we use the previously defined function **fact** as an argument to **apply3**.

```
ML> apply3 (fact);
    6 : int
```

Any function with the right type—ones with an integer argument—can be used by **apply3**.

```
ML> apply3 (fn x => x+16);
    19 : int
```

```
ML> apply3 (fn x => ({a=x},  true));
    ({a=3}, true) : {a:int} * bool
```

The most useful source of higher-order functions comes from reoccurring structure of other functions. Consider the similarities in the following two function definitions.

```
ML> fun
..> incr (nil)  = nil |
..> incr (h::t) = (h+1) :: incr (t);
   val incr = [function] : int list -> int list
```

```
ML> fun
..> half (nil)  = nil |
..> half (h::t) = (h/2.0) :: half (t);
   val half = [function] : real list -> real list
```

Both functions perform some operation on every element of the list and produce a new list of the same length made up of all the results. In the first case the operation is `(fn x=>x+1)`; in the second case `(fn x=>x/2.0)`. If one, or the other, of these functions were bound to the global identifier **f** we might write the following:

```
ML> val f = (fn x=>x+1);
    val f = [function] : int -> int
```

```
ML> fun incr (list) =
 ..>  case list of
 ..>    nil => nil |
 ..>    h::t => f(h) :: incr (t);
    val incr = [function] : int list -> int list
```

We just have to abstract over the function **f** by adding it as an argument to arrive at the following version of the function we call **map**.

```
ML> fun map (f,list) =
..>  case list of
..>    nil => nil |
..>    h::t => f(h) :: map (f,t);
    val map = [function] : ('a -> 'b) * 'a list -> 'b list
```

We say the operation "maps" or "applies" its function argument to every element of the list. This is a familiar function to LISP programmers where it is known as MAPCAR and to those acquainted with Backus' FP as α. The function **map** can be used to define **incr** or **half**, or used directly on lists to map the appropriate function on every element of the list.

```
ML> map (fn x=>x+1, [1,2,3,4,5]);   (* "map" sucessor func to list *)
    [2,3,4,5,6] : int list

ML> fun incr (list) = map (fn x=>x+1, list);
    val incr = [function] : int list -> int list;

ML> incr [1,2,3,4,5];                       (* new incr behaves as before *)
    [2,3,4,5,6] : int list
```

Similarly, **half** can be defined using **map**.

```
ML> map (fn x=>x/2.0, [2.0, 3.0, 4.0]);
    [1.0, 1.5, 2.0] : real list

ML> fun half (list) = map (fn x=>x/2.0, list);
    val half = [function] : real list -> real list;

ML> half [2.0, 3.0, 4.0];
    [1.0, 1.5, 2.0] : real list
```

Another useful function for manipulating lists can be derived by considering the common structure of these two functions.

```
ML> fun
..>   gt0 (nil) = nil |
..>   gt0 (h::t) = if h>0 then h::gt0(t) else gt0(t);
    val gt0 = [function] : int list -> int list

ML> fun
..>   eqsq (nil) = nil |
..>   eqsq (h::t) = if h*h=h then h::eqsq(t) else eqsq(t);
    val eqsq = [function] : int list -> int list
```

Both of these functions filter a list of integers, discarding those elements not having some property. This property can be represented by a boolean function and passed as an argument to another function that does the filtering. We define the function **filter** as follows:

```
ML> fun filter (f,l) =
..>    if null l
..>       then []
..>       else if f(hd l)
```

```
..>       then (hd l)::(filter (f, tl l))
..>       else filter (f, tl l);
   val filter = [function] : (('a -> bool) * 'a list) -> ('a list)
```

Alternatively, we may define **filter** by case analysis.

```
ML> fun
..>   filter (f,nil) = nil |
..>   filter (f,head::tail) =
..>      if f(head)
..>        then head::(filter (f, tail))
..>        else filter (f, tail);
   val filter = [function] : (('a -> bool) * 'a list) -> ('a list)
```

By passing the function **filter** different boolean functions as arguments, different sublists of a list can be obtained. For example, we get the elements greater than zero, and those elements equal to their square using the two following function calls:

```
ML> filter ((fn x => x>0), [~1,0,1])
   [1] : int list

ML> filter ((fn x => x*x=x), [~1,0,1])
   [0,1] : int list
```

4.4.2 Returning Functions

We have emphasized that ML treats function objects no differently from all the other values in the language. Because subprocedures can return integers, subprocedures may also return functions. In this section we give examples of functions that return functions as their value.

One simple example of returning functions is the function **const** that returns the constant function.

```
ML> fun const (x) = (fn y => x);
   val const = [function] : 'a -> 'b -> 'a
```

This function takes an argument **x** (of any type) and returns a function. This function is a function that ignores its argument and always returns the same value—namely, **x** the value passed to **const**. Note that **const** is not a constant function; the value it returns is a constant function.

The following function returns a binary function. It returns either the plus function or the times function.

```
ML> fun f(x) = if x<1 then (fn (y,z) => y+z) else (fn (y,z) => y*z);
    val f = [function] : int -> (int * int -> int)
```

Consider the type of the expression **f(2)**. It is **int*int->int**. So **f(2)** is a function and as a function it can be applied to arguments.

```
ML> f (2);
    [function] : int*int->int

ML> f (2) (5,8);
    40 : int

ML> f (~1) (5,8);
    13 : int
```

The last two expressions are once again suggestive. If **f** can be used like **f** arg_1 arg_2, why not define **f** like **f** pat_1 pat_2? This is indeed possible. Not only is it quite natural, but it also saves symbols by avoiding the anonymous **fn** construct. The function **f** rewritten this way looks like the following:

```
ML> fun f (x) (y,z) = if x<1 then y+z else y*z;
    val f = [function] : int -> (int * int -> int)
```

One function-returning function, usually called **fold**, is often useful. We give its definition as a further example of higher-order function definitions.

```
ML> fun fold f l x =
..>    if null(l)
..>       then x
..>       else f (hd l, fold f (tl l) x);
    val fold = [function] : ('a * 'b -> 'b) -> ('a list) -> 'b -> 'b
```

This function applies the binary function **f** to elements of the list starting from the end. The next function also applies a binary function to elements of the list but starts at the front of the list.

```
ML> fun revf f l x =
..>    if null(l)
..>       then x
..>       else revf f (tl l) (f (hd l, x));
    val revf = [function] : ('a * 'b -> 'b) -> ('a list) -> 'b -> 'b
```

The composition of functions is another good example. Composition is most naturally viewed as an operation on functions. As a higher-order function it takes two input functions and returns a third function.

```
ML> fun comp (f,g) = (fn x => f (g (x)));
    val comp = [function] : (('a -> 'b) * ('c -> 'a)) -> ('c -> 'b)
```

This is equivalent to the following:

```
ML> fun comp (f,g) (x) = f(g(x));
    val comp = [function] : (('a -> 'b) * ('c -> 'a)) -> ('c -> 'b)
```

We can use the function **comp** to compose two filters together to form a new one.

```
ML> comp (gt0, eqsq);
    [function] : int list -> int list
```

If we had written **filter**

```
ML> fun
..>  filter f (nil)       = nil |
..>  filter f (head::tail) =
..>   if f(head) then head::(filter f tail) else filter f tail;
   val filter = [function] : ('a -> bool) -> 'a list -> 'a list
```

then **comp(gt0,eqsq)** could have been written

```
ML> filter (fn x => x>0 andalso x*x=x);
    [function] : int list -> int list
```

This second version of **filter** is called the *curried* version of the function in honor of Haskell Brooks Curry (1900–) who noted that functions with multiple arguments could be eliminated in this way in favor of higher-order functions. Sometimes it is convenient to curry functions in this way to facilitate their use in different contexts.

Higher-order functions can be partially applied to their arguments. We begin by defining a higher-order function **times**, which multiplies two integers. In contrast to the usual binary definition, **times** takes one integer as an argument and returns a function that also takes one integer as an argument. Here are three equivalent ways of defining **times**.

```
ML> val times = (fn x => (fn y => x * y));
    val times = [function] : int -> (int -> int)
```

```
ML> fun times (x) = (fn y => x * y);
    val times = [function] : int -> (int -> int)
```

```
ML> fun times (x) (y) = x*y;
    val times = [function] : int -> (int -> int)
```

Now we multiply two numbers together.

```
ML> times 3 4;
    12 : int

ML> times 2;
    [function] : int -> int
```

The expression **times 2** is not an integer product but a function.
    The function **times** may be used in yet other function definitions.

```
ML> val twice = times 2;      (* Func twice define w/o using vars *)
    val twice = [function] : int -> int

ML> twice 5;                  (* Example use of twice.            *)
    10 : int
```

The function **fourtimes** can likewise be defined without using the **fun**
function binding or the anonymous **fn** form. In particular, no formal argument
names are required in the definition. The function **fourtimes** can be defined
using **twice** and the composition function **comp** defined earlier.

```
ML> val fourtimes = comp (twice, twice);      (* Defined w/o vars *)
    val fourtimes = [function] : int -> int

ML> fourtimes 5;              (* Example use of fourtimes.        *)
    20 : int
```

    The function **times** computes the same function as the built-in function
*, yet it has a different type. It does not require a pair of numbers as an
argument.

```
ML> times;
    [function] : int -> (int -> int)

ML> op *;
    [function] : (int * int) -> int
```

(The keyword **op** is used in ML to alert the parser that the following infix
(binary) operation is not being used as usual between two operands.)
    This process of currying a binary function is a function itself. We define
this function in ML as it is an interesting higher-order function. The function
curry is an object just like any other. To emphasize the point we define the
function **curry** with an ordinary value binding.

```
ML> val curry = (fn f => (fn a => fn b => f(a,b)));
    val curry = [function] : (('a * 'b) -> 'c) -> ('a -> ('b -> 'c))
```

As a function object it can be written more succinctly using the **fun** function
binding.

```
ML> fun curry (f) (a) (b) = f(a,b);
    val curry = [function] : (('a * 'b) -> 'c) -> ('a -> ('b -> 'c))
```

To see the use of the **curry** function we define the ordinary binary
plus function.

```
ML> fun plus (x,y) = x + y;
    val plus = [function] : (int * int) -> int
```

The curried version of the **plus** function can be obtained by applying the
function **curry** to **plus**.

```
ML> val curryplus = curry plus;
    val curryplus = [function] : int -> (int -> int)
```

Notice the resulting function **curryplus** is a higher-order function.
The same currying can be applied to the built-in addition function, as
long as the infix status of the symbol **+** is considered.

```
ML> val curryplus = curry (op +);
    val curryplus = [function] : int -> (int -> int)
```

The value of a curried function is that it can be applied to some of its
arguments.

```
ML> val successor = curryplus 1;
    val successor = [function] : int -> int
```

Of course, it is not possible to directly apply a binary function to only
one of its arguments.

```
ML> val succ = plus 1
Type error -- Domain of function does not match argument.
The function is plus
Its domain is    int * int
The argument is 1
Its type is      int
```

The only way to accomplish this is to introduce a new function.

```
ML> fun succ = (fn x => plus (1,x))
    val succ = [function] : int -> int
```

Notice we must introduce a formal argument **x**. In effect the **curry** function already provides this service without requiring a new function.

We have already pointed out that application is left associative. Consequently, the following two expressions are the same.

```
ML> fold (fn x => 1) [2,3] 4;
    1 : int
```

```
ML> ((fold (fn x => 1)) [2,3]) 4;
    1 : int
```

The arrow type operator, incidentally, is right associative. That is to say that **t->s->r** means **t->(s->r)**. This associativity has the pleasing consequence that the type of a partial application can be easily determined. Assume we have **f** of type **t->s->r**, which is equivalent to **t->(s->r)**, and **a** of type **t**, and **b** of type **s**. The following shows the relationship between partial application and types of the resulting expressions:

$$
\begin{array}{rl}
\textbf{f} & \textbf{:t->s->r = t->(s->r)} \\
\textbf{f a} \; : & \textbf{s->r} \\
\textbf{(f a) b =} \; \textbf{f a b} \; : & \textbf{r}
\end{array}
$$

4.5 FUNCTION BINDINGS

To summarize we give the syntax of function bindings:

fun $id\ pat_{11} \ \ldots\ pat_{1n} = exp_1 \ | \ \ldots\ | \ id\ pat_{m1} \ \ldots\ pat_{mn} = exp_m$

The ... is not part of the syntax. The reader is left to imagine the m rows of n patterns each.

Function binding is a derived form, because it is a special case of a recursive value binding. The preceding function binding is equivalent to the following value binding:

```
val rec id = (fn x₁ => ... fn xₙ =>
  case (x₁, ..., xₙ) of
    (pat₁₁, ..., pat₁ₙ) => exp₁
    | ... |
    (patₘ₁, ..., patₘₙ) => expₘ)
```

The formal parameter names $x_1, \ldots, x_n$ must be names that are different from the identifiers in the original function binding.

■ Chapter 5

User-defined Data Types

In this chapter we will introduce ways the user can build new types. In these type definitions we will need to be able to write type expressions. We have already seen many type expressions, because ML prints one for every expression the user types to the system. They are formed from the base types (**int**, **bool**, **real**, **string**, and **unit**) using all the type operators associated with the different kinds of data structures introduced in previous chapters.

	Value	Type
tuples	(*exp*, ..., *exp*)	*type* ***** *type* ***** *type*
records	{*l* = *exp*, ..., *l* = *exp*}	{*l* : *type*, ..., *l* : *type*}
lists	[*exp*, ..., *exp*]	*type* **list**
functions	**fn** *id* **=>** *exp*	*type* **->** *type*

For example, **bool list -> int** is a type expression—the type of functions from lists of boolean values to integers. In some cases parentheses are required in type expressions to ensure that the type operators apply to the right argument. For example, **int*(real->string)** is one type expression, and **int*real->string** is an entirely different one. There are an infinite collection of these type expressions. But this collection does not include all the types the programmer may desire, like enumerated types or trees, to name just two.

Above and beyond the collection of predefined types, ML has a mechanism for the user to add new types distinct from the built-in collection. The new type may be parameterized by other types, like the built-in type **'a list**, in this case the new type is really a user-defined type operator, and an infinite collection of separate types can be built, all of which use the new type operator. Each type introduces a collection of constructors to build elements of the type. These constructors join all the predefined constructors in being used with pattern matching. The new type has elements that resemble the terms in a free term algebra. Therefore, we call these types *algebraic*.

Algebraic data types can be defined in two ways in ML. The functions that construct the elements of a new type can be public. This is a concrete type. An abstract type hides the constructors, thus protecting the representation of the type. This ensures controlled access to the type. In the next few sections we give examples of these two kinds of type definitions, as well as introduce type abbreviations and give some more substantial ML programs employing user-defined data types.

5.1 CONCRETE TYPES

Concrete types are introduced by the keyword **datatype**. The type name is given, and then one or more ways are given to construct the type. Here is a common special case of the syntax for concrete type definitions.

‹type binding› ::=
    datatype *‹type name›* = *‹constructor binding›* | . . . | *‹constructor binding›*

Each constructor binding is separated by the | character. This single ML **datatype** definition subsumes many diverse data type definitions found in other languages, like enumerated types, variant records, and pointers to types, as we shall see.

We give an example of an enumerated type representing the primary colors. In this case each constructor binding consists of merely the name of a new constructor.

```
ML> datatype Color = Red | Yellow | Blue;
    datatype Color
    con Red : Color
    con Yellow : Color
    con Blue : Color

ML> Blue;
    Blue : Color
```

Color is an enumerated type with three elements. **Red, Blue, Yellow** are constructors, and as such they can be used in patterns. Like all constructors they are values too; in this case they are really 0-ary functions or constants.

The data type for boolean values is another example of an enumerated type. Its definition could be given as follows:

```
ML> datatype bool = true | false;
    datatype bool
    con true : bool
    con false : bool
```

Of course, the data type **bool** is predefined in the ML system, so there is no need to define it. This does show how versatile the algebraic type-defining mechanism is, however. Definitions of **not** and **or** for the data type **bool** follow:

```
ML> fun not (true) = false | not (false) = true;
    val not = [function] : bool -> bool
```

Because **true** and **false** are constructors, they can be used as patterns. In particular, they can be used in function definitions like **not**. Next we define the infix function for disjunction.

```
ML> infix 6 or;
    symbol "or" given infix status (left assoc, precedence=6).

ML> fun
..>    true or true   = true |
..>    false or true  = true |
..>    true or false  = true |
..>    false or false = false;
    val or = [function] : bool * bool -> bool
```

The function **not** is predefined in the ML system. However, the function **or** is not. This function has the same truth table as the ML **orelse** construct. But the **orelse** construct is not a function; it does not evaluate both its arguments unless necessary. The function **or** defined earlier is equivalent to the following definition:

```
ML> fun x or y = x orelse y;
    val or = [function] : bool * bool -> bool
```

A data-type definition may only have one constructor.

```
ML> datatype one = one;
    datatype one
    con one : one;
```

This type has exactly one element and is isomorphic to the predefined type **unit**. Notice that we have used the type name as the name of the only constructor. Because type and constructor identifiers do not share the same name space this is legal. There must be at least one constructor binding, however, in a **datatype** declaration. If there were no constructors, there would be no elements of the type, and this would be pointless. However, it is possible (although still pointless) to define a user-defined type with no elements.

All the previous examples have been of constructors with arity zero. The special case of 0-ary or constant constructors yields the enumerated types. Other types can be built using *n*-ary constructors. These constructors require a constructor binding using the keyword **of**.

> *<constructor binding>* ::= *<constructor name>* of *<type>*
> *<constructor binding>* ::= *<constructor name>*

As we have seen, the "of *<type>*" phrase is optional in a constructor binding. Here is an example of a concrete data type with the **of** part.

```
ML> datatype Shape =
..>    Rectangle of real * real    |
..>    Circle of real              |
 .>    Line of (real * real) list  |
..>    Spline of (real * real) list;
    datatype Shape
    con Rectangle : real * real -> Shape
    con Circle : real -> Shape
    con Line : (real * real) list -> Shape
    con Spline : (real * real) list -> Shape
```

Here is a long list of values of type **Shape**.

```
    Circle (1.2)
    Circle (3.1)
    Rectangle (2.7, 3.2)
    Rectangle (3.3, 2.1)
    Line ([])
    Line ([(1.1, 2.3)])
    Line ([(1.1, 2.3), (5.2, 9.1)])
    Line ([(1.1, 2.3), (5.2, 9.1), (4.5, 3.9)])
    Spline ([])
    Spline ([(1.1, 2.3)])
```

```
Spline ([(1.1, 2.3), (5.2, 9.1)])
Spline ([(1.1, 2.3), (5.2, 9.1), (4.5, 3.9)])
```

Constructors can have elements of any types as arguments including functions. The following is an example of a constructor **con** that takes an integer function as an argument.

```
ML> datatype T = con of int -> int
    datatype T
    con con : (int -> int) -> T

ML> fn x => 3;                    (*  Not an element of type T.    *)
    [function] : 'a -> int

ML> con (fn x => 3);              (*  Example element of type T.  *)
    con ([function]) : T
```

The types of the last two expressions are not the same. It is a common mistake to ignore or forget the constructor, especially when there is just one, which coerces the representation of the type to the type itself.

The scope of the constructor is always the same as that of the type being defined.

```
ML> local
..>    datatype T = con1 of int | con2 of real;
..> in
..>    fun
 .>      f (con1 n) = 0|
..>      f (con2 r) = 1;
..> end;
    val f = [function] : T -> int
```

The scope of the function **f** extends beyond the scope of the type of its argument. In this example the function **f** cannot be called, because no elements of type **T** can be constructed.

5.1.1 Recursive Type Definitions

Type definitions can be recursive. All that is necessary is to mention the type being defined in one of the constructor bindings; no different syntax is used (like **val** and **val rec**). Data type definitions are all implicitly recursive as any other interpretation is hardly ever useful. A binary tree is a perfect example of a recursive data structure.

```
ML> datatype Tree = empty | node of int * Tree * Tree;
    datatype Tree
    con empty : Tree
    con Node : (int * Tree * Tree) -> Tree
```

All the constructor bindings may use the name of the type being declared to denote the resulting type. The two constructors of type **Tree** are **empty** and **node**. Here is a list of values of type **Tree**.

```
empty
node (1, empty, empty)
node (2, node (1, empty, empty), empty)
node (3, empty, node (1, empty, empty))
node (4, node (1, empty, empty), node (1, empty, empty))
```

In a language like Pascal or Ada the programmer would be forced to use pointers for a data type like the preceding one, because recursive types are forbidden. Programming with pointers is susceptible to errors and requires the management of allocation and deallocation of storage for the data structures.

Here is another recursive type declaration.

```
ML> datatype T = con of T;
    datatype T
    con con : T -> T
```

This time no elements of type **T** can be constructed, because to construct one with the constructor **con** requires that an element of **T** already exist. Conversely, this following kind of declaration is occasionally useful.

```
ML> datatype T = con of T list;
    datatype T
    con con : T list -> T
```

Elements of type **T** include the following:

```
con []
con [con []]
con [con [], con []]
con [con [], con [], con []]
con [con [con [], con []], con [con []], con []]
```

The empty list has to occur to initiate the construction of an element of the type, and the empty list is a list of any type.

The liberal mechanism to define recursive type encourages one to challenge Cantor's theorem and build a type isomorphic to its function space. Cantor proved with his famous diagonalization argument that this is not possible as the cardinality of the function space must be strictly greater.

```
ML> datatype T = con of T -> T;
    datatype T
    con con : (T -> T) -> T
```

A function of type **T->T** like **(fn x=>x)** is not an element of type **T**, however.

```
ML> con (fn x => x);
    con ([function]) : T
```

Thus, self-application has been avoided.

```
ML> (fn x:T => x x);
Type error -- Attempt to build a self-referential type.
  The function:  x
  Its argument:  x
```

However, it is still possible to write a function that loops endlessly.

```
ML> fun f (x as con g) = g x;
    val f = [function] : T -> T
```

Notice that the function **f** itself is not recursive.

Mutually recursive types, like mutually recursive functions, are defined using the keyword **and**. Here is an example of mutually recursive types suggesting the imperative constructs of statements and blocks.

```
ML> datatype
..>   Stmt = assign | block of Block;
..> and
..>   Block = begin of Stmt list;
    datatype Stmt
    con assign : Stmt
    con block : Block -> Stmt
    datatype Block
    con begin : Stmt list -> Block
```

The data type **Stmt** is composed of the element **assign**, which is to suggest an assignment statement, and blocks. Blocks are made to be statements by the constructor **block**. The data type **block** is simply a list of statements.

Neither data type can be defined separately as each depends on the other. Here are some elements of type **Stmt**.

```
assign
block (begin [assign])
block (begin [assign, assign])
block (begin [assign, block (begin [assign]), assign])
```

Here are some elements of type **Block**.

```
begin [assign]
begin [assign, assign]
begin [assign, block (begin [assign]), assign]
```

5.1.2 Type Operations

The built-in type operations like * (cartesian product) or -> (function space) are not the only type operations. The user can define new type operators. One of these type operators that can be defined is the union operator. This is the "tagged" union operator, as each element must be explicitly injected into one "side" or the other. Here is the definition of the **Union** type operator.

```
ML> datatype ('a,'b) Union = InLeft of 'a | InRight of 'b;
    datatype ('a,'b) Union
    con InLeft : 'a -> (('a,'b) Union)
    con InRight : 'b -> (('a,'b) Union)
```

Here now are some examples using elements of the **Union** type.

```
ML> InLeft (3);  InRight (true);
    InLeft 3 : (int,'a) Union
    InRight true : ('a,bool) Union

ML> InLeft (3) = InRight (true);
    false : bool

ML> InLeft (3) = InRight (3);
    false : bool
```

The following function sums the integers of a union type.

```
ML> fun
..>    sum (nil)              = 0                    |
```

```
..>    sum (InLeft(n)::rest)  = n + sum(rest) |
..>    sum (InRight(_)::rest) = sum(rest)      ;
    val Sum = [function] : (int, 'a) Union list -> int
```

Notice that the type **Union** is not as flexible as we might wish. The function **Sum** works on all **Union** types if the integer values are injected on the left. If they are injected on the right, they are ignored. It is impossible to define an ML function that tests the type of an object as in the following hypothetical function definition:

```
fun f (x) = if x:int then x else 0
```

The intention is that if the argument to **f** is an integer then **f** returns this value, otherwise the value of **f** is zero. One can argue that the function **f** is reasonable for arguments of all types, **int**, **real**, lists, and so on. Hence, **f** should be polymorphic. But this requires a radical departure from the philosophy of strong typing. The type of all objects would have to be maintained during run time to implement the test of the object's type.

5.2 TYPE ABBREVIATIONS

It is possible to introduce new names for types that act as an abbreviation for a type expression.

```
ML> type IntPair = int * int;
    type IntPair = int * int
```

The newly introduced type name can be used wherever a type can be used and is structurally equivalent to the type on the right-hand side of the equals symbol.

Names for types can include arguments—type variables. These variables stand for any type. Like all type operators the name comes after the arguments.

```
ML> type ('a,'b) Pair = 'a * 'b;
    type ('a,'b) Pair = 'a * 'b

ML> type ('a,'b) A_List = ('a * 'b) list;
    type ('a,'b) A_List = ('a * 'b) list;

ML> type A_List = ('a * 'b) list;
Semantic error -- Unbound type variables in type abbreviation.
```

Another pitfall is that type abbreviations are not recursive.

```
ML> type  T = int * T;
Semantic error -- Undefined type constructor 'T'.
```

The only purpose of type abbreviations is to make it easier to write certain types that may appear often in an ML program. Internally the ML system ignores the names of the type abbreviations in determining the types of expressions. Unfortunately, the system cannot always know which name the user might wish to associate with a particular type as this is not necessarily unique.

Take for example the situation in which both feet and meters are represented as integers.

```
type Feet = int;
type Meters = int;
```

Now any integer can be considered as an element of type **Feet** or **Meters**.

```
ML> 3 : Feet;
   3 : int

ML> 4 : Meters;
   4 : int
```

This sort of structural type equivalence is not popular in modern strongly typed conventional programming languages. These languages tend to favor name equivalence to avoid unintentional mixing of types that coincidentally have the same representation. Name equivalence can easily be obtained in ML by using the **datatype** construct.

```
datatype Feet = Feet of int and Meters = Meters of int
```

The cost of this approach is that integers are not elements of type **Feet** or type **Meters**. They must be explicitly coerced by the appropriate constructor. But, of course, that is inherent in the demand that the compiler keep the values of the different types separate for the programmer.

5.3 ABSTRACT TYPES

Abstract types provide an interface for the use of elements of some type. By limiting access to the representation of a type for the users of the type, the provider of the type can present an abstraction concerning the nature of the type that cannot accidentally be pierced. In ML the access to the representation of a type is entirely through the constructors. The constructors of the type create the elements and decompose them as well. By limiting the scope of the type constructors to the type definition itself, the type definer can create an abstract type. Apart from the access to the type, the nature of an abstract type is the same as concrete types. They are both algebraic types.

The form of an abstract type definition in ML is as follows:

```
abstype T = R
with
    :
    :
end
```

The scope of the constructors declared in R is between the keywords **with** and **end**. Any collection of declarations is legal between the keywords **with** and **end**. This includes **val** bindings, **fun** bindings (actually a special case), other type bindings, and exception bindings (see the next chapter).

There is no point in having an **abstype** for lists, say. The concrete type

```
datatype 'a list = nil 1 cons of 'a * 'a list
```

is appropriate, because the representation of lists does not need protection for any reason. If one defined an abstract type for lists, one would have to reveal the constructors immediately for programmers to build lists.

```
ML> abstype 'a List = Nil' | Cons' of 'a * 'a list
..> with
..>   val Nil = Nil';
..>   val Cons = Cons';
..> end;
    abstype 'a List
    val Nil = [abs] : 'a List
    val Cons = [abs] : 'a * 'a List -> 'a List
```

Even this is not enough. Defining **Nil** and **Cons** as an abstract type in this way makes them *functions* and not *constructors*. So **Nil** and **Cons** *cannot* be used in pattern matching, so destructors are required as well.

```
abstype 'a List = Nil' | Cons' of 'a * 'a list
with
  fun Null Nil = true | _ = false;
  fun Hd (Cons' (a,_)) = a;
  fun Tl (Cons' (_,l)) = l;
  val Nil = Nil';
  val Cons = Cons';
end;
```

The conclusion is that an abstract type is unnecessary in the case of lists.

One reason an **abstype** is needed is to protect the internal representation of a data structure or maintain it in a consistent state. Such is the case for types that cannot be viewed as algebraic data structures. An example is the type for graphs. We wish to provide the interface for the following operations on graphs.

```
val nodes     : 'a Graph -> 'a list
val empty     : 'a Graph
val add_edge  : 'a * 'a * 'a Graph -> 'a Graph
val is_edge   : 'a * 'a * 'a Graph -> bool
```

In the ML **abstype** that follows directed graphs are represented by a list of adjacency lists. Each node *N* is followed by a list of the nodes for which there is a directed edge from *N*.

```
abstype 'a Graph = graph of ('a * 'a list) list
with
  fun nodes (graph l) = map #1 l;      (*  all nodes in graph       *)
  val empty = graph [];                (*  the graph with no nodes  *)
  local    (* add an edge to a graph    *)
    fun
      f (a,b,nil) = [(a,[b])] |
      f (a,b,(a',adj)::rest) =
        if a=a' then (a,b::adj)::rest else (a',adj)::f(a,b,rest);
    fun g (a,b,l) =
      let
        val ex = exists (fn x => x=b) (a::(map #1 l));
        val l' = f (a,b,l);
      in
        if ex then l' else (b,nil)::l'
      end;
  in
    fun add_edge (a,b,graph l) = graph (g (a,b,l));
  end;

  local  (* determine if an edge is in a graph  *)
    fun
      f (b,nil)      = false               |
      f (b,b'::rest) = b=b' orelse f(b,rest) ;
    fun
      g (a,b,nil)              = false                                   |
      g (a,b,(a',adj)::rest)=if a=a' then f(b,adj) else g(a,b,rest);
  in
    fun is_edge (a,b,graph l) = g (a,b,l)
  end;
end;
```

Not every element of type (**'a*'a list) list** represents a graph. For example, the following do not:

```
[(1, [2])]
[(1, [2]), (1, [3])]
```

The first list has a node in the graph, namely **2**, that does not have an adjacency list. The second list has two adjacency lists for the same node. The function **add_edge** goes to some length to avoid creating a list that does not represent a graph. The following table lists some graphs and their representation.

Graph	Representation
add_edge(1,2,empty)	[(2,[]), (1,[2])]
add_edge(1,3,add_edge(1,2,empty))	[(3,[]), (2,[]), (1,[2,3])]

We next consider another common data structure, one that associates values with keys. We call this data structure an *association list*. This important and often used structure is known by many different names: a-list (in LISP programming), table (in the Icon programming language), dictionary, and symbol table. We have chosen to implement an association list as a list of pairs in the following example. In some cases it may be helpful to view an association list as an abstract type with two simple operations: "look up" the value of a key and "update" the value associated with a key. This interface is conceptually simpler than the interface to a list of pairs, which is cluttered by a myriad of possibilities.

```
abstype ('a,'b) Assoc = assoc of ('a * 'b) list
with
  exception not_found;
  local
    fun
      lookup' (x, nil)        = raise not_found |
      lookup' (x, (y,z)::rest) = if x=y then z else lookup' (x, rest);
  in
    fun lookup (x, assoc A) = lookup' (x, A)
  end;

  fun update (a, b, assoc A) = assoc ((a,b)::A);

  val empty = assoc nil;
end;
```

The constructor **assoc** is local to the functions defined with the abstract type. The functions that are visible after the preceding declaration are **lookup**, which searches the data structure for the right key, and **update**, which adds another pair to the data structure. Also defined are **empty**, the empty data structure, and the exception **not_found** (exceptions are introduced in chapter 6). In the next examples we build up a list that associates strings with numbers.

```
ML>  val a = update (3, "three", empty);
     val a = [abstype] : (int, string) Assoc

ML>  val b = update (2, "two", a);
     val b = [abstype] : (int, string) Assoc
```

The system does not print the structure of an element of an abstract type; the structure is not available to the programmer.

```
ML>  update (4, 4+3, b);
Type error -- Domain of function does not match argument.
The function is update
Its domain is    int * string * (int, string) Assoc
The argument is (4, 4+3, b)
Its type is      int * int * (int, string) Assoc

ML>  lookup (2, b);
     "two" : string
```

Another, entirely plausible, implementation for association lists is one that uses functions, not lists.

```
abstype ('a,'b) Assoc = assoc of ('a -> 'b)
with
  exception not_found;
  fun lookup (x, assoc A) = A x;
  fun update (a, b, assoc A) =
    assoc (fn x => if x=a then b else A x);
  val empty = assoc (fn x => raise not_found);
end;
```

Both implementations provide the user the same abstract interface or environment, namely, the identifiers:

```
exception not_found
val lookup : 'a * ('a,'b) Assoc -> 'b
```

```
val update : 'a * 'b * ('a,'b) Assoc -> ('a,'b) Assoc
val empty : ('a,'b) Assoc
```

Modules (see chapter 9) can serve the same purpose of encapsulating an interface or environment.

5.4 ABSTRACT SYNTAX

Although the syntax for defining data types is so simple that it hardly needs any examples, a significant portion of the effort of solving substantive programs in ML centers around the design of data types. So, in this section we demonstrate the use of ML data types in expressing the abstract syntax of language. We use these definitions later when we discuss the algorithm for type checking the ML programming language.

We begin with a data structure for expressions of a vastly simplified version of the programming language ML.

```
type Variable =  string;
datatype Expr =
    Var of Variable           |   (* formal parameters    *)
    Num of int                |   (* integer numerals     *)
    Bln of bool               |   (* boolean values       *)
    Fun of Variable * Expr    |   (* function definition   *)
    App of Expr * Expr        |   (* function application *)
    Cond of Expr * Expr * Expr;   (* if construct          *)
```

Every value of type **Expr** corresponds to an ML expression in this simple subset of the real language. The following table gives some examples. These examples are all syntactically legal but not necessarily type correct.

Element of Expr	Simple ML Expression
Num 17	17
Bln true	true
Fun ("x", Var "x")	(fn x => x)
App (Fun ("x", Var "x"), Num 4)	(fn x => x) 4
Cond (Bln true, Num 0, Num 1)	if true then 0 else 1
Cond (Num 0, Fun("x",Num 1), Bln false)	if 0 then (fn x=>1) else false

The last line in the table corresponds to an expression that is not type correct. It is not correct for two reasons. First, the expression tested does not have boolean type. Second, the types of the expressions in the branches of the conditional are not the same.

Each value **v** of type **Expr** can be viewed as a tree. The nodes would be labeled with the name of the constructors, and the subtrees are the arguments to the constructor. This tree corresponds closely with the usual parse of the ML expression represented by **v**.

Corresponding to the data structure for expressions, we have a data structure for type expressions. We include only the types we need for the expressions defined in **Expr**.

```
type TypeVariable = string;
datatype Type =
   TypeVar of TypeVariable |   (* type variables    *)
   Bool                    |   (* boolean type      *)
   Int                     |   (* integer type      *)
   Arrow of Type * Type    ;   (* type of functions *)
```

This **datatype** definition corresponds to the following BNF grammar for types.

<type> ::= <type variable>
<type> ::= bool
<type> ::= int
<type> ::= <type> -> <type>

In words, this grammar defines a type to be a type variable, a type constant **bool** or **int**, a function type, or a list type. The grammar gives a concrete syntax for the language of types. The ML data structure gives an abstract representation of type expressions.

Any BNF definition (or context-free grammar) can be represented as an ML data type by picking a constructor for each rule. In the preceding example, the two unstructured types each have their own 0-ary constructor. The arrow type, which requires a type for the domain and a type for the range, is represented by a binary constructor; each argument is another element of the type **Type**. Type variables are themselves types, and this is represented by a unary constructor that coerces type variables to the type **Type**.

This makes ML especially suitable for the meta-language in denotational semantics of languages. Using ML this way has the pleasing result that the definition is, in fact, an interpreter for the language. An extended example can be found in one of the references [18].

5.5 EXAMPLE PROGRAM: INTERPOLATION
BY POLYNOMIALS

With ML functions (discussed in the last chapter) and user-defined data
structures (the subject of this chapter), it is now possible to write more
substantial ML programs. In this section we take an example from the field of
numerical analysis.

Suppose that we are interested in approximating the values of some
function f, given only a limited set of points (x_i, y_i) where $y_i = f(x_i)$. These
points can be used to define a polynomial $P(x) = a_0 + a_1 x + a_2 x^2 + \cdots + a_n x^n$
that approximates the function f. Then we can evaluate the polynomial P at
any points of interest. We adopt this strategy, and we apply it to interpolating
some values of the inverse tangent function. We begin by defining a general
data structure for polynomials with real-valued coefficients.

We represent a polynomial by a list of pairs. This representation is
protected by making the data structure an **abstype**. The only way the user is
permitted to make a polynomial is term by term using the function **term**, or by
adding and multiplying existing polynomials. This controlled access protects,
for instance, the unique representation of the zero polynomial. The only other
function provided by the abstract type for polynomials is **eval**, to evaluate a
polynomial given a real number.

```
type Exp  = int;      (* exponent     *)
type Coef = real;     (* coefficient  *)

abstype Poly = poly of (Exp * Coef) list
with
   (*  exp and coef make up a term which is a poly  *)
   fun term (e,c) = if c=0.0 then poly [] else poly [(e,c)];

   (*  evaluate a polynomial at a particular value  *)
   local
       fun exp (r: real, n)   = if n<=0 then 1.0 else r * exp(r,n-1);
       fun eval' r ((e,c), x) = c*(exp(r,e)) + x;
   in
       fun eval (poly m) (r: real) = fold (eval' r) m 0.0;
   end;

   local
     fun
       add' ((a,n:Coef),nil)         = if n=0.0 then [] else [(a,n)] |
       add' (one as (a,n:Coef),(b,m)::t) =
         if a=b
           then if n+m=0.0 then t else (a,n+m)::t
           else (b,m) :: add' (one,t);
```

```
fun tm' (e:Exp,c:Coef) (a,m) = (e+a,c*m);

fun
   mult' (_,nil)  = nil   |
   mult' (nil,_)  = nil   |
   mult' (h::t,1) = fold add' (map (tm' h) 1) (mult' (t,1));
in
   (*  add two polynomials  *)
   fun add (poly m, poly 1) = poly (fold add' m 1);

   (*  multiply two polynomials  *)
   fun mult (poly m, poly 1) = poly (mult' (m, 1));
end;
end;
```

For convenience we define two more functions using the abstract data type for polynomials just given. These functions are used several times in the remainder of the program.

```
fun const x  = term (0,x);                   (* constant polynomial  *)
fun xminus x0 = add (term (1,1.0), term (0, ~x0)); (* poly: (x-x0)  *)
```

Now we write a program to compute a polynomial—that is, an element of the **Poly** abstract type. We observe that a set of n points uniquely determines a polynomial of degree $n-1$. We wish to write a function **N** that takes a list of n points as input and returns the polynomial going through those points. This polynomial is given by the Newton interpolation formula

$$P_0 = y_0$$

$$P_{01...n} = P_{01...(n-1)} + d_{01...n}(x - x_0)(x - x_1)\cdots(x - x_{n-1})$$

where the coefficients $d_{01...n}$ are the divided differences given by the following inductive definition:

$$d_i = y_i$$

$$d_{i(i+1)...k} = \frac{d_{(i+1)...k} + d_{i(i+1)...(k-1)}}{(x_k - x_i)}$$

The definition of the divided differences requires the addition, multiplication, and division of real numbers. Notice that the definition of $P_{01...n}$ requires the addition and multiplication of polynomials. The following ML program **N** calculates the approximating polynomial $P_{01...n}$ given a list of points.

```
local
   (*  divided differences                   *)
   fun
```

```
    dd (nil)        = 0.0      |
    dd ((x,y)::nil) = y        |
    dd (l) =
      let
        val l' = rev l;
        val x0 = (#1 (hd l));   val xn = (#1 (hd l'));
        val a  = dd (tl l) - dd (rev (tl l'));
      in
        a/(xn-x0)
      end;

  (*  poly:   (x-x0)(x-x1) ... (x-xn)  *)
  fun
    pp (nil)   = const 1.0                |
    pp (x0::t) = mult (xminus x0, pp t) ;
in
  (*  Newton interpolation formula     *)
  fun
    N (nil)         = const 0.0 |
    N ((x,y)::nil) = const y    |
    N (l)           =
      let
        val l' = rev (tl (rev l));
      in
        add (N l', mult (const (dd l), pp (map #1 l')))
      end;
end;
```

We intend to use the function **N** to approximate the inverse tangent function which we define and call **f**. The definition of **f** is given in the next few lines.

```
local
  val pi = 3.141592653589793;
  fun torad (x) = (pi * x) / 180.0;
  fun cot x = (cos x) / (sin x);
in
  fun f x = cot (torad x);
end;
```

We use **f** to calculate the values of the inverse tangent on a list of five points.

```
val data = map (fn x => (x, f x)) [1.0,2.0,3.0,4.0,5.0];
```

Now the ML expression **N(data)** is a polynomial approximating the inverse tangent function. On the values

```
val v = [1.0, 1.5, 2.0, 2.5, 3.0, 3.5, 4.0, 4.5, 5.0]
```

the polynomial evaluates to

```
[57.2899616307595, 39.2329136110775, 28.6362532829156,
 22.6351915819588, 19.0811366877282, 16.5416940235814,
 14.3006662567120, 12.3580532981499, 11.4300523027614]
```

using the ML expression **map (eval (N data)) v**. These values differ
from those computed by **f** by

```
[2.1E~14, 1.0, 2.5E~14, ~0.2, ~2.1E~14, 0.2, 3.7E~14, ~0.3, 5.2E~14]
```

respectively. The difference on the given points is quite small and due to
arithmetic errors; after all the polynomial is supposed to be exactly equal to **f**
on these points. The difference at the other values is actually quite significant,
however.

For this function and set of points it is possible to do better by
approximating **f** with a rational polynomial defined as the ratio of a pair
of polynomials. So we will extend this example to a second approach
for approximating functions. The following definitions build a new type
Rat_Poly and operations for rational polynomial. These definitions take
advantage of the abstract type **Poly** already defined.

```
type Rat_Poly = (Poly * Poly);

infix 7 //;  (* division of rational polynomials *)
infix 6 ++;  (* addition of rational polynomials *)

fun (p1,q1)++(p2,q2) = (add (mult(p1,q2), mult(p2,q1)), mult(q1,q2));
fun (p1,q1)//(p2,q2) = (mult (p1,q2), mult (p2,q1));

fun eval_rat (p,q) x = (eval p x) / (eval q x);
fun const_rat x = (const x, const 1.0);
```

A rational polynomial has a polynomial for the numerator and a polynomial
for the denominator. The operations on rational polynomials are obvious
generalizations. We require the capability of evaluating a rational polynomial
eval_rat, which evaluates both numerator and denominator, then divides.
We also require addition and division of rational polynomials. These operators
are defined earlier and given the infix names **++** and **//**, respectively.
For convenience we define **const_rat**, which creates a constant rational
polynomial.

For a given set of points a rational polynomial can be obtained in several ways. Thiele's continued fraction polynomial is given by $Q_{01...n}(x) = Q_{01...n}^n$ where

$$Q_{01...n}^0 = 0$$

$$Q_{01...n}^i = \frac{(x - x_{n-i})}{\phi_{01...(n-i+1)} + Q_{01...n}^{i-1}}$$

for $n \geq 2$ and $0 \leq i \leq n$. The value of $\phi_{01...n}$ is given by $\phi_{01} = \rho_{01}$ and $\phi_{01...n} = \rho_{01...n} - \rho_{01...(n-2)}$ where

$$\rho_\epsilon = 0$$

$$\rho_i = y_i$$

$$\rho_{i...k} = \frac{(x_i - x_k)}{\rho_{i...(k-1)} - \rho_{(i+1)...k}} + \rho_{(i+1)...(k-1)}$$

The following ML program Q calculates the approximating rational polynomial given a list of points.

```
local
  fun
    rho (nil)        = 0.0 |
    rho ((x,y)::nil) = y   |
    rho (l) =
      let
        val l'  = rev l;         val l'' = rev (tl l');
        val x0  = (#1 (hd l));   val xn  = (#1 (hd l'));
        val a   = (rho l'') - (rho (tl l));
      in
        (x0-xn)/a + (rho (tl l''))
      end;

  fun phi l = (rho l)-(rho (rev (tl (tl (rev l)))));

  fun f (x0) = (xminus x0, const 1.0);  (* rat poly:  (x-x0)  *)

  (*  Thiele's continued fraction  *)
  fun
    Q' (_,nil) = const_rat 0.0                                 |
    Q' (nil, (x,y)::rest) = (const_rat y) ++ Q' ([(x,y)],rest) |
    Q' (x0i,xi12n) =
      let
        val (xi,_) = hd (rev x0i);
        val x0i1   = x0i @ [(hd xi12n)];
      in
        (f xi) // (const_rat (phi x0i1) ++ Q' (x0i1, tl xi12n))
      end;
```

```
in
  fun Q l = Q' (nil, l);
end;
```

On the values

```
[1.0, 1.5, 2.0, 2.5, 3.0, 3.5, 4.0, 4.5, 5.0]
```

the rational polynomial Q(data) differs from f by

```
[0.0, 1.2E~7, ~3.6E~15, ~2.7E~8, 3.6E~15,
 1.4E~8, 0.0, ~1.9E~8, ~1.8E~15]
```

In this case the rational approximation is much better—accurate to six places right of the decimal. Even at the given points, the values yielded by Q(data) are better than the polynomial N(data).

■ Chapter 6

Exception Handling

Sometimes the course of computation takes a rare or abnormal turn. For example, a matrix program may calculate that the determinate of a matrix is zero, or a compiler may detect a syntax error in the input. The normal sequence of events is disrupted, and some other action must be undertaken to repair the problem, or, if that is not possible, then give up entirely. A well-written program does not ignore these problems nor does it permit the auxiliary actions to disturb the clean presentation of the normal flow events. Good programming language constructs can facilitate writing programs that deal with exceptional events.

Many of these events are caused by input that is not wanted. Although the ML type system guarantees that a program will always receive data of the advertised type, sometimes this is not enough. For example, integer division works for all integer divisors *except* zero. The function **sqrt** works for all real arguments that are not negative. What possibilities are there for these situations? One possibility is to relinquish control to the operating system of the computer, as in the case of a divide-by-zero interrupt in an assembly language. This is undesirable, however, because it takes control of these events out of the programmer's explicit control. A second possibility is to define arbitrary values for these functions on those troublesome inputs. In the case of dividing by zero, one might arbitrarily select a very large integer as the resulting value. But what values should be chosen, and how can the programmer distinguish a normal value from a conventional value?

The solution in ML is to return special constructors called exceptions at any point in the program in the place of the normal value. Raising an exception signals that an abnormal event transpired. Programs can detect and trap these exceptions, and take different actions accordingly. This exception-handling facility resembles the catch and throw mechanisms in LISP. It also has similarities with the exception-handling facility in the Ada programming language.

6.1 PREDEFINED EXCEPTIONS

A function, instead of returning a value, may signal some abnormal condition. For example, the built-in division function indicates division by zero whenever the divisor is zero. Further execution halts, and ML prints a message to the user at the top level.

```
ML> 2 div 0;                    (* division by zero is not defined    *)
UNCAUGHT EXCEPTION -- Div
```

The ML system responds by indicating that an exception was raised, and the system prints the name of the exception. In this case the quotient of the **div** function was zero, so an integer result was not returned. Instead an exception named **Div** was raised. Usually the program does not contain a zero quotient explicitly but would contain the possibility of a zero quotient, as in the next example. Here the function **f** may or may not return zero depending on the input value.

```
ML> fun f(n) = if n=4 then 0 else 1;
    val f = [function] . int => int

ML> 3 div f(4);  (* division by zero is possible here, if f(4)=0  *)
UNCAUGHT EXCEPTION -- Div
```

Of course, division does not always raise an exception. In fact, the raising of a **div** exception is (presumably) unusual.

Most of the predefined exceptions are named for the operation that can cause the exception to be raised. This is a good indication of what happened, because it is usually obvious what input values cause problems for some particular operation. Here are two examples.

```
ML> ln 0.0;      (* logarithm of 0 is not defined              *)
UNCAUGHT EXCEPTION -- Ln

ML> sqrt ~2.0;   (* square root of a negative number is not real  *)
UNCAUGHT EXCEPTION -- Sqrt
```

The exceptions **Div**, **Ln**, and **Sqrt** are predefined exceptions known to the ML system. So we must be careful to distinguish between the identifier

div standing for the division function and the identifier **Div** standing for the exception raised when the divisor is zero. Because exceptions occupy the same name space as values and constructors, the names of the exceptions cannot be identical with the operations. By convention the exception names are capitalized.

Some important built-in exceptions are **Match** and **Bind**. These exceptions originate from pattern matching in value bindings (section 3.3) and function definitions (section 4.2.1). If the run-time value of an object cannot be decomposed in a way required by a pattern, then the exception **Bind** is raised. Here is an example:

```
ML> datatype T = con1 of int | con2 of real
    datatype T
    con con1 : int -> T
    con con2 : real -> T

ML> val con1 (n) = con2 (2.3);
UNCAUGHT EXCEPTION -- Bind
```

A similar situation occurs with functions. Consider the following function definition, which does not cover all the possibilities for the data type **T**:

```
ML> fun f (con1 n) = n;
Semantic warning -- Patterns not exhaustive in def'n of function f.
    val f = [function] : T -> int

ML> f (con2 (2.3));
UNCAUGHT EXCEPTION -- Match
```

The ML system must give a warning when compiling any function that might raise the exception **Match**.

There are some unusual events that have exceptions of their own. One of these is the **Interrupt** exception, which is raised if the ML program is interrupted by the user during its execution. Another one of these is the **Alloc**[1] exception, which is raised if the execution of the program exhausted available memory. Because the ML system performs garbage collection as needed, the **Alloc** exception is rare.

6.2 EXCEPTION HANDLING

Exceptions can be trapped before they reach the top level. This permits the computation of an alternative value for an expression should it raise an exception. The syntax of the trapping mechanism has a handler after the

---

[1] This is not part of the definition of Standard ML [12].

expression that may signal an exception. An exception handler is indicated by
the keyword **handle**. An arrow indicates the expression to be evaluated in
the event an exception is indicated. The syntax for a handler is as follows:

exp_1 **handle** _ => exp_2

The alternative expression exp_2 is evaluated and its value returned as the value
of the whole expression only if the evaluation of exp_1 results in an exception
being raised. Of course, the type of exp_1 and exp_2 must be the same, since
the value of either one might be returned as the value of the whole expression.
Here is an example.

```
ML> (16 div 0) handle _ => 45;
    45 : int
```

In the preceding example, the evaluation of the expression **(16 div 0)** causes
the exception **Div** to be raised. This exception is caught by the handler, and
the value **45** is returned. In the syntax of the preceding exception handler,
the underscore (the wild-card pattern) indicates that any exception, no matter
which one, will be caught. In the next example the handler catches the **Sqrt**
exception.

```
ML> (sqrt ~2.3) handle _ => 3.5;
    3.5 : real
```

Other forms of an exception handler can be selective about which
exceptions are to be caught. These forms replace the underscore by the name
of the exception to be handled.

```
ML> (7 div (2-2)) handle Div => 45;
    45 : int

ML> (7 div (2-2)) handle Sqrt => 45;
UNCAUGHT EXCEPTION -- Div

ML> sqrt (ln 0.0) handle Div => 9.99E9
UNCAUGHT EXCEPTION -- Ln

ML> sqrt (ln 0.0) handle Sqrt => 9.99E9
    9.99E9 : real
```

If the exception raised is different from the one that is named in the handler,
then it is as if the handler was not there at all.

Handlers can be generalized to trap any one of several exceptions. The general form for these handlers is as follows:

exp `handle` *exn*$_1$ => *exp*$_1$ | *exn*$_2$ => *exp*$_2$ | ... | *exn*$_n$ => *exp*$_n$

Each case is separated by |. There is an alternative expression for each exception. The appropriate expression is evaluated should the expression *exp* raise an exception. The following is an example of a multiple handler.

```
ML> (1 div 0) handle Sqrt => 1 | Ln => 2 | Div => 3;
    3 : int
```

The wild-card pattern can be used as an "others" or default case. This means that all other exceptions not explicitly named in the earlier cases will be handled.

```
ML> (1 div 0) handle Sqrt => 1 | Ln => 2 | Div => 3 | _ => 4;
    3 : int
```

6.3 USER-DEFINED EXCEPTIONS

The programmer can initiate as well as handle exceptions. An exception is initiated by the **raise** statement. The syntax is

    `raise` *exn*

where *exn* is the name of some exception. For example,

```
ML> raise Div;
UNCAUGHT EXCEPTION -- Div

ML> if 1=2 then raise Sqrt else 4;
    4 : int

ML> if 1=1 then raise Sqrt else 4;
UNCAUGHT EXCEPTION -- Sqrt
```

Of course, raising a predefined exception capriciously can be misleading, because one normally associates dividing by zero with the exception **Div** and taking the square root of a negative number with **Sqrt**. As we will demonstrate shortly, the user can define other exceptions to signal whatever events are deemed necessary. Naturally only exceptions, not other values, can be raised with the **raise** statement. If the expression is not an exception, an error is reported.

```
ML> raise div;
Type error -- Expression raised is not an exception.
The expr: div
Its type: int * int -> int
```

The identifier **div** denotes the integer division operator. This operator is not an exception (**Div** is), and so cannot be raised.

User-defined exceptions are introduced by a declaration of the form

    exception *exn*

where *exn* is the name of the new exception. This is another example of a binding. We have already discussed value bindings in chapter 3, the special case of function bindings in chapter 4, and type bindings in chapter 5. There is no value appearing in an exception binding, as in value bindings, because an exception binding of this form is a request for an entirely new exception object. The nature of this object is not important; it is just a signal distinct from any others.

The scope of exception bindings is governed by the same rules as value bindings. There are top-level bindings and local bindings. Declaring an exception at the top level is the way to cause the exception to be visible in the rest of the session. The following is an example of an exception declaration of NonPos followed by a function that raises **NonPos** if its argument is negative or zero; otherwise it subtracts one.

```
ML> exception NonPos;     (* Declare an exception called "NonPos". *)
    exception NonPos

ML> fun f (n) = if n>0 then n-1 else raise NonPos;
    val f = [function] : int -> int
```

The function **f** applied to a nonpositive argument causes the **NonPos** exception to be raised. The user-defined exception **NonPos** can be caught or not at the programmer's discretion.

```
ML> f(4);
    3 : int

ML> f(~4);
UNCAUGHT EXCEPTION -- NonPos
```

If it is desired that a conventional value be returned when the input is less than or equal to zero, then a handler can be used. The function does not have to be changed in any way.

```
ML> f(~4) handle NonPos => 0;
    0 : int
```

Alternatively, a new function can be defined with the property of returning the conventional value.

```
ML> val g (n) = f(n) handle NonPos => 0;
    g = fun : int -> int

ML> g(4);   g(~4)
    3 : int
    0 : int
```

The following is an example of a local exception binding.

```
ML> local
..>    exception e             (* Declare an exception called "e". *)
..> in
..>    val h (n) = if n>0 then n-1 else raise e
..> end;
    h = [function] : int -> int
```

Trying to catch the exception defined in a local declaration is a problem. It is possible to catch the exception along with all other exceptions, as in the following example:

```
ML h(~4) handle _ => 0;
    0 : int
```

It is not possible, however, to catch this exception by name because its scope was confined to the local definition of the function **h**.

```
ML> h(~4) handle e => 0;
Semantic error -- The identifier e is undefined.
```

Nor is it possible to raise this exception (other than by calling the function **h**).

```
ML> raise e;
Semantic error -- The identifier e is undefined.
```

The handlers and the **raise** statements must all be in the scope of any exception they mention. Of course, this is true of all identifiers. The unique property of exceptions is that their handling follows the dynamic chain.

6.3.1 Exception Propagation

When an exception is raised the appropriate handler must be found. The handlers in the next two examples have no effect. (The function **g** was defined earlier.)

```
ML> g(~4) handle NonPos => ~1;    (*  NonPos caught by g already.  *)
    0 : int

ML> g(~4 handle NonPos => ~2);
    0 : int
```

In this last example, the evaluation of **~4** does not cause an exception to be raised, so the handler for **NonPos** just given has no effect on the computation, but the handler for **NonPos** in the function **g** does catch the exception raised by the evaluation of **f** applied to **~4**. The search for the appropriate handler follows the run-time stack of currently pending subprograms.

The following example illustrates another problem in finding the right exception handler. It is tempting to write a common exception handler like **h** with the intention of using it in several places when this kind of exception handling is required.

```
ML> fun h x = x handle Div => 3;
    val h = [function] : int -> int
```

Unfortunately, the function **h** is useless.

```
ML> h (4 div 0)
UNCAUGHT EXCEPTION -- Div
```

The evaluation of the actual argument to **h** raises an exception; hence, the function **h** is never executed. The program calling **h** must deal with the exception.

An exception can propagate outside its static scope, as illustrated by the function **f** defined subsequently.

```
ML> fun f (x) =
..>    let exception TooBig in
..>       if x > 100 then raise TooBig else x+1
..>    end;
    val f = [function] : int -> int
```

For arguments less than a hundred, the function raises no exception. For large arguments, however, the function raises the exception **TooBig**, which is declared locally to the body of the function **f**. Because the exception is not handled locally, the exception is propagated along the dynamic chain and outside the static scope of **TooBig**.

```
ML> f(50);
    51 : int;
```

```
ML> f(101);
UNCAUGHT EXCEPTION -- TooBig
```

In other words, the user cannot type the identifier **TooBig** and mean the same exception named **TooBig**, which has propagated to the top level.

Here is a more captious example.

```
ML> exception TooBig;
    exception TooBig
```

```
ML> f(101) handle TooBig => 5;
UNCAUGHT EXCEPTION -- TooBig
```

The exception named **TooBig** that is handled in the preceding handler is not the same exception that is declared local to the function **f**, even though they have the same name. Hence, the handler did not trap the exception **TooBig** raised within the function **f**, and it is propagated to the top level. The only way to handle an exception that has propagated outside of its lexical scope is to use a catch-all clause in the handler.

```
ML> f(101) handle TooBig => 1 | _ => 2;
    2 : int
```

Just like value bindings, there are local, global, and multiple exception bindings. We have illustrated local and global exception bindings earlier. Now we give an example of a multiple exception binding that ascertains the order of evaluation of expressions in a tuple.

```
ML> exception LeftToRight and RightToLeft;
    exception LeftToRight
    exception RightToLeft
```

```
ML> (raise LeftToRight, raise RightToLeft);
UNCAUGHT EXCEPTION -- LeftToRight
```

Depending on which expression is evaluated first, one or the other of the exceptions will be raised. In the ML system described here, a tuple is evaluated

left to right, so the exception **LeftToRight** is raised ending the evaluation
of the tuple.

6.3.2 Nongenerative Exception Bindings

Value bindings compute some value and bind it to an identifier. Exception
declarations usually create an object called an exception. The exception object
is a completely new thing that did not exist before. Thus, we call the exception
declarations *generative* exception bindings. It is possible to bind an exception
identifier to an old exception object, although this is relatively rare. Such a
binding has the following form:

exception exn_1 = exn_2

where exn_1 and exn_2 are two identifiers, names of exceptions. The exception
exn_2 must be defined already. In the following example the exception **e2** is just
another name for the exception denoted by **e1**.

```
ML> let
..>    exception e1;
..>    fun f () = let exception e2=e1 in raise e2 end;
..> in
..>    f() handle e1=>1 | _=>2
..> end;
    1 : int
```

Just as in the case of value binding, the branches of multiple exception
bindings are independent, so

```
ML> exception e1 and e2 = e1;
Semantic error -- The exception e1 is undefined.
```

is not only pointless, but illegal, if the identifier **e1** has not previously been
bound to an exception.

Exception bindings are not recursive. So the following is possible, but it
is difficult to imagine that any useful program could take advantage of this fact.

```
ML> local
..>    exception e
..>    fun f () = let exception e = e in raise e end;
..> in
..>    f() handle e => 1 | _ => 2;
..> end;
    1 : int
```

6.3.3 Exceptions in Recursive Programs

In this section we look at the situation that arises with exception handling in recursive programs. We begin by defining the following recursive function:

```
ML> fun f(n) =
..>    let
..>       exception e
..>    in
..>      if n mod 2 = 0
..>        then f (n div 2) handle e => n
..>        else if n mod 3 = 0
..>           then (n div 3)
..>           else raise e
..>    end;
   val f = [function] : int -> int
```

This function divides even numbers by two and calls itself recursively. On numbers divisible by three, but not by two, this function divides the input by three. On all other numbers the function raises the exception **e**.

```
ML> f(3);
   1 : int;

ML> f(6);
   1 : int;

ML> f(5);
UNCAUGHT EXCEPTION -- e
```

If the recursive call to the function raises the local exception **e** it is not caught by a handler for **e** in any preceding invocation of the function. The local exceptions are distinct in different invocations of the function **f**.

```
ML> f(14);                   (* NB.  Not handled by handler  *)
UNCAUGHT EXCEPTION -- e
```

In fact, the handler defined in the function **f** is useless; it cannot handle any exception.

The semantics here is deliberate—a binding local to a function is independent in every invocation of the function. This is certainly what is expected in value bindings. For instance, in

```
ML> fun f (n) = let val x=n-1 in if n<2 then 1 else n*f(x) end;
   val f = [function] : int -> int
```

the value of **x** is the appropriate one for a particular invocation of **f**. It does not transcend the invocation.

   Conversely, the programming language Ada requires that the exception created locally in a recursive program is the same exception regardless of the invocation of the function—in effect making the exception global to the function yet visible only in the function body. This can be achieved easily in ML using a local declaration. The preceding example would be changed to the following:

```
ML> local
..>    exception e
..> in
..>    fun f(n) =
..>      if n mod 2 = 0
..>        then f (n div 2) handle e => n
..>        else if n mod 3 = 0
..>          then (n div 3)
..>          else raise e
..> end;
    val f = [function] : int -> int
```

Here the exception binding for the exception **e** is not local to the function **f**. In this case the handler does catch exceptions raised by other invocations of the function **f**. Some cases are the same.

```
ML> f(3);
    1 : int

ML> f(6);
    1 : int

ML> f(5);
UNCAUGHT EXCEPTION -- e
```

In other cases the handler will catch the exception before it propagates to the top level.

```
ML> f(14);
    14 : int
```

6.4 EXCEPTIONS WITH VALUES

Not only can an exception be raised, indicating an abnormal event has transpired, but also a value can be associated with the exception. This is integrated into the language by making exceptions constructors. As some values are formed by applying constructors to arguments, the same syntax is used to associate values with exceptions. The purpose of these values is to furnish additional information about the circumstances in which the exception is raised. This information can be an object of any ML data type. The declaration of an exception can indicate the type of the additional information. The form is as follows:

> **exception** *exn* **of** *type*

The type of an exception must be a monotype.

```
ML> exception e of int;    (* Associated with exception is an int. *)
    exception e

ML> fun f (n) = if n>0 then n-1 else raise e(n)
    val f : int -> int

ML> f (~3);
UNCAUGHT EXCEPTION -- e (~3)
```

6.4.1 Example

We consider a more lengthy example to illustrate some of the possibilities of raising exceptions with values.

```
exception Prime of int;
exception TooBig of int * int;

local
  val primes = [2,3,5,7,11,13,17,19,23,29,31,37,41,43,47,53,59,61];
  val max = hd (rev primes)
  fun f (n,h::t) =
    if n < h*h
      then raise Prime(n)
      else if n mod h <= 0 then h else f(n,t);
in
  fun LeastPrimeFactor (n) =
    if n<max then f(n,primes) else raise TooBig(n,max)
end;
```

The function **LeastPrimeFactor** checks if a number is prime or not. If the input is not prime, it returns the smallest prime factor. If the number is prime, an exception **Prime** is raised with the prime number. The function **LeastPrimeFactor** can only test numbers up to a certain size, which depends on the given list of prime numbers. If the input is too large, then the function raises an exception **TooBig** with the input and the maximum value.

6.4.2 Discriminating among Values Raised with Exceptions

Exception handlers can discriminate not only among the exceptions raised but also on the values raised with an exception. If no value is raised by an exception, then a branch of the exception handler has the form we have seen.

exn => *exp*

The language takes advantage of exceptions as constructors and generalizes exception handling to include patterns. If the value returned by the handler is to depend on the value raised with the exception, then the branch of the exception handler has the form:

exp **handle** pat_1 => exp_1 | pat_2 => exp_2 | ... | pat_n => exp_n

As exceptions are constructors of type **exn**, they are legal constitutions of patterns. These patterns must all have the type **exn**, and so these patterns all have exception identifiers at the outermost position of the term. Some may have other patterns as arguments. This is exactly like function application. In this case, the "argument" is the value raised with the exception *exn*.

```
ML> exception e of int;
    exception e

ML> fun f (n) = if n mod 2 = 0 then n div 2 else raise e (n);
    f = fun : int -> int

ML> val g (n) =
..>    f(n) handle
..>       e(0) => 0 |
..>       e(1) => 1 |
..>       e(m) => if m mod 3 = 0 then m div 3 else 99
..>    ;
    g = fun : int -> int

ML> g(2); g(5); g(9);
    1 : int
    99 : int
    3 : int
```

An exception handler may raise an exception itself. Here we redefine **g** to reraise the exception **e**.

```
ML> fun g (n) =
..>    f(n) handle
..>       e(0) => 0 |
..>       e(1) => 1 |
..>       e(m) => if m mod 3 = 0 then m div 3 else raise e(m)
..>    ;
    g = fun : int -> int
```

Even if the exception name is not in the scope of handler the program fragment **x=>raise x** will catch every exception and then reraise it. This is useful so that a function can complete unfinished actions (e.g., close files) in the event the computation is halted by the raising of an unhandled, perhaps unexpected, exception.

```
ML> fun g (n) =
..>    f(n) handle
..>       e(0) => 0          |
..>       e(m) => if m mod 3 = 0 then m div 3 else 99 |
..>       Div => 98          |
..>       Alloc=> 97
..>    ;
    val g = [function] : int -> int
```

6.4.3 Constrained Exception Bindings

In this section we explain why global exception bindings must be constrained by monotypes. The section can be skipped by the incurious reader. A similar problem occurs with references. See section 8.2.

Suppose that we allowed exceptions to have types with type variables in them. For instance, assume that we declare an exception **e** to have type **'a**.

```
ML> exception e of 'a;          (*  NOT LEGAL *)
    exception e
```

Then both of the following functions would presumably be legal:

```
ML> fun f (n) = if n mod 2 = 0 then n div 2 else raise e(99);
    val f = [function] : int -> int
```

```
ML> fun g (n) = if n mod 3 = 0 then n div 3 else raise e("string");
    val g = [function] : int -> int
```

Now consider the situation when both functions are used simultaneously.

```
ML> fun h (n) = (f(n), g(n));
```

```
h = [function] : int -> int * int
```

```
ML> h(6);
    (3, 2) : int * int
```

```
ML> h(4);                        (* HYPOTHETICAL *)
UNCAUGHT EXCEPTION -- e("string")
```

```
ML> h(3);                        (* HYPOTHETICAL *)
UNCAUGHT EXCEPTION -- e(99)
```

Now we design a handler for the exception **e**.

```
ML> fun i (n) = h (n) handle e(v) => (v+1,v+2);
    val i = [function] : int -> int * int
```

What is the type of variable **v** in the handler? If it is **'a**, then presumably we can specialize it to type **int** so that we can add to it. But this is not possible, since a string value could be returned as the value of the exception **e**. The problem cannot arise if the values raised with an exception have the same monotype in all contexts.

6.5 EXCEPTION AS VALUES

Exceptions are implemented as constructors of a special predefined type **exn**. The type **exn** is different from other user-defined data structures defined with the **datatype** construct in that the programmer may continually add new constructors (exceptions) to the **exn** type. So exceptions are values, although there are no operations on them. We will see in this section that it is possible to take advantage of the fact that exceptions are values, as well as to write some peculiar programs.

Here is a function that raises its argument.

```
ML> fun f (x) = raise x;
    val f = [function] : exn -> 'a
```

As this function never returns a value, the type of the return value can safely be assumed to be any type whatsoever.

The following example illustrates a common misconception about exception values. Here we try to catch the argument as an exception, or viewed another way, we abstract over the exception name in the handler.

```
ML> fun g x = 1 handle x => 2;
    val g = [function] : 'a -> int
```

This does not work as may have been intended. Notice the type of **h**. The first argument is unconstrained, not **exn**. This is because the two appearances of **x** are unrelated. Both, not just the first appearance, are patterns binding the appropriate value to the variable **x**. In the first case this value is the actual argument; in the second case it is the exception value raised (if any). This is exactly analogous to the following **case** statement.

```
ML> fun g x = case 1 of x => 2;
    val g = [function] : 'a -> int
```

Here is an example using exceptions with exceptions as values.

```
ML> exception X of exn;
    exception X of exn

ML> fun f (x) =
..>    let
..>       exception Neg and Pos;
..>    in
..>       if x<0 then raise X(Neg) else if x>0 then raise X(Pos) else 0
..>    end;
    val f = [function] : int -> int

ML> fun g (x) = f (x) handle X(y) => raise y;
    val g = [function] : int -> int
```

The function **g** raises an exception passed to it as the value raised with the exception **X**, if **X** is raised.

We have discussed functions, user-defined data structures, and exceptions. With these three elements it is possible to program more realistic ML functions. In the final two sections of this chapter we give examples of more substantive ML programs.

6.6 EXAMPLE PROGRAM: SELECTION WITHOUT REPLACEMENT

Jon Bentley discusses the following problem in the "Programming Pearls" column in the *Communications of the ACM*, December, 1984:

> The input consists of two integers M and N, with $M < N$. The output is a sorted list of M random numbers in the range $1 \ldots N$ in which no integer occurs more than once.

Donald Knuth gave a well-documented solution written in a combination of TEX and Pascal. An ordered hash table is used to solve the problem efficiently when *M* is reasonably large yet small compared with *N*. Half of the program/documentation is devoted to this sophisticated data structure. Another part of the program gets the input values *M* and *N* from the user interactively.

In this section we provide an ML solution to this problem. We ignore obtaining the input as ML is already interactive, and we solve the problem using a simpler data structure, a binary search tree.   This data structure is more suitable for the nonimperative part of ML than is the hash table.

```
datatype 'a tree = empty | node of 'a * 'a tree * 'a tree;
```

We must provide the capability to insert elements into the tree.

```
exception equal;
fun
  insert (x, empty)  = node (x, empty, empty) |
  insert (x, node (y,l,r)) =
    if (x<y)
      then node (y,insert(x,l),r)
      else if (x=y)
        then raise equal
        else node (y,l,insert (x,r))   ;
```

The function **insert** adds an element to the tree. We are interested in keeping these elements distinct, so an exception is raised if an element is already in the tree.

Among the operations that one might want to perform on a binary search tree, we require only the ability to list the nodes using an in-order traversal.

```
fun
  in_order (empty) = nil |
  in_order (node (x,l,r)) = (in_order l) @ [x] @ (in_order r);
```

The function **f** performs the selection without replacement. It calls on the function **g** to do the work after checking the arguments. The function **f** initializes the binary search tree.

```
exception bad_input;

local
    (*  Add a random number 1..n to the binary search tree S;  if the
        number is already there, then try again.              *)
    fun add (n,S) = insert (random n, S) handle equal => add (n,S);
    (*  Keep adding to S for m times; return the nodes in order.    *)
    fun g (n,m,s,S) =
      if s=m then in_order S else g (n, m, s+1, add(n,S))
in
```

```
    fun f (n,m) =
      if n<=0 orelse m<0 orelse m>=n
        then raise bad_input
        else g(n,m,0,empty)
end;
```

The function **random** returns a random integer in the range one to *n*. This function is not described here. The language constructs necessary to build a function to generate random numbers are introduced in chapter 8.

6.7 EXAMPLE PROGRAM: KLONDIKE

The final example of this chapter is a sample ML program to play the popular solitaire card called Klondike. This game is played with a standard deck of fifty-two cards. We will represent a card as a record in ML.

```
type Value = int; (*  really 1=ace, 2, 3,  ..., 12=queen, 13=king  *)
datatype Suit = spades | hearts | diamonds | clubs;
type Card = {suit:Suit, value:Value};
```

The cards are laid out in a tableau of seven piles with one, two, three, four, five, six, and seven cards, respectively. The remainder of the cards are kept aside and examined card by card as the game progresses. The object of the game is to sort the deck into four piles—one for each suit. These piles are called the foundation. The layout for the game is captured in the following data structure:

```
type Pile = (Card list * Card list);

type Layout = {
  foundation : Value * Value * Value * Value,
  tableau : Pile list,    (* list of length 7 easier than 7-tuple *)
  stock : Card list * Card list
};
```

A significant design decision has been made regarding the representation of the tableau. A 7-tuple might be considered more natural than a list to represent the tableau, because the tableau is of fixed size, but it is easier to perform the same operation on lists using recursion than to manipulate each element of the 7-tuple individually. So we choose to represent the tableau as a list.

The function **init** takes a deck of cards (presumably shuffled) and initializes the tableau.

```
(*  set up the initial layout for Klondike.  *)
local
  exception Split;
  local     (*  divide a list in two:  1, ..., n, and n+1, ..., 1  *)
    fun
      split' (0,x,y)   = (rev x, y)  |
      split' (n,x,nil) = raise Split |
      split' (n,x,h::t)= split' (n-1,h::x,t);
  in
    fun split n l = split' (n,nil,l);
  end;
in
  fun init (deck: Card list) : Layout =
    let
      val rest = deck;
      val (p1,rest) = split 1 rest;
      val (p2,rest) = split 2 rest;
      val (p3,rest) = split 3 rest;
      val (p4,rest) = split 4 rest;
      val (p5,rest) = split 5 rest;
      val (p6,rest) = split 6 rest;
      val (p7,rest) = split 7 rest;
    in {
      (*  initially no cards are played on the foundation.  *)
      foundation = (0,0,0,0),
      (*  turn 1 card over in each pile.  *)
      tableau = map (split 1) [p1,p2,p3,p4,p5,p6,p7],
      (*  turn 1 card over from the stock to the discard pile.  *)
      stock = split 1 rest
    } end;
end;
```

The game is played until all the cards are arranged in sequence on the foundation. The function **win** recognizes when the layout is complete. Moves in the game of Klondike often depend on the color and value of the cards, and the function **compat** checks when cards have opposite color and are in sequence.

```
(*  win=true iff configuration has fully built foundation.      *)
fun
  win {foundation=(13,13,13,13),
       tableau=_,        (*  ignore tableau; should be all empty.  *)
       stock=(nil,nil)} = true |
  win _ = false;

(*  a card can be played on another card if they have
    opposite colors and their values are in sequence.            *)
```

```
local
  fun
    opp (spades,   s) = (s=hearts orelse s=diamonds) |
    opp (clubs,    s) = (s=hearts orelse s=diamonds) |
    opp (_,        s) = (s=spades orelse s=clubs)    ;
in
  fun
    compat ({suit=s1,value=v}, {suit=s2,value=w}) =
      v+1=w andalso opp (s1,s2);
end;
```

The function **add** adds a card to the foundation in the appropriate place, if it is possible. Otherwise it raises the exception **Match**. We use this extreme measure of raising a predefined exception as we view the functions representing the moves of the game as patterns that may fail to match the layout if the move is not possible.

```
fun
  add {suit=spades,value=v}  (s,h,d,c) =
    if s+1=v then (v,h,d,c) else raise Match |
  add {suit=hearts,value=v}  (s,h,d,c) =
    if h+1=v then (s,v,d,c) else raise Match |
  add {suit=diamonds,value=v}(s,h,d,c) =
    if d+1=v then (s,h,v,c) else raise Match |
  add {suit=clubs,value=v}   (s,h,d,c) =
    if c+1=v then (s,h,d,v) else raise Match ;
```

The legal moves of the game of Klondike are divided into six categories. Each category of move is implemented by a separate function that transforms the layout to the new position, if a move is possible, or, if the move is not applicable, raises the exception **Match**. The following table summarizes the legal moves of the game:

Move	Description
promote	Play a card on the foundation from the discard pile.
build	Play a card on the foundation from the tableau.
turn	Uncover the top card on some pile in the tableau.
stack	Move a stack from one pile on the tableau to another.
get	Play a card on the tableau from the discard pile.
new	Turn over a new card from the stock.

The following short function uses **add** (which can raise the· exception **Match**) to move card **cd** from the stock to the foundation.

```
(*  Add to foundation from the stock.  *)
fun
  promote {foundation=f,tableau=p,stock=(cd::r,left)} =
    {foundation=add cd f, tableau=p, stock=(r,left)};


(*  Build on the foundation from the tableau.  *)
local
  fun
    g nil f s ps                        = raise Match |
    g ((p as (cd::x,y))::rest) f s ps = (
      {foundation=add cd f, tableau=(rev ps) @ ((x,y)::rest), stock=s}
        handle Match =>g rest f s (p::ps)
    ) |
    g (p::rest) f s ps = g rest f s (p::ps);
in
  fun
    build {foundation=f,tableau=p,stock=s} = g p f s nil;
end;


(*  Turn over a card, if no cards are face up on a pile.  *)
local
  fun
    turn' nil                 = raise Match         |
    turn' ((nil,cd::r)::rest)= (cd::nil,r)::rest |
    turn' (p::rest)           = p::(turn' rest)    ;
in
  fun
    turn {foundation=f, tableau=t, stock=s} =
      {foundation=f, tableau=turn' t, stock=s};
end;


(*  Move an entire stack to another pile.  *)
local
  exception no_place;
  fun
    g (s,nil)      = raise no_place |    (* nothing left to try.  *)
    g ((nil,x),t) = raise no_place |    (* nothing to move.       *)
    g ((x,nil),(nil,nil)::t) =           (* nothing to uncover.    *)
      if #value(hd(rev x))=13
        then raise no_place
        else (nil,nil)::(g((x,nil),t)) |
    g ((x,y),(nil,nil)::t) =             (* king goes on empty pile.*)
      if #value(hd(rev x))=13
        then (x,nil)::t
```

```
          else (nil,nil)::(g((x,y),t))    |
  g (p,(nil,u)::t) =(nil,u)::(g(p,t))|(* need to turn card over.*)
  g ((x,y),(u,v)::t)=
    if compat (hd (rev x), hd u)
      then (x@u,v)::t
      else (u,v)::(g((x,y),t));
fun
  stack' nil    = raise Match    |
  stack' (h::t) =
    (nil,#2 h)::(g (h, t)) handle no_place => h::(stack' t);
fun stack'' t = stack' t handle Match => (rev (stack' (rev t)));
in
fun
  stack {foundation=f, tableau=t, stock=s} =
    {foundation=f, tableau=stack'' t, stock=s};
end;


(* Get a card from the stock pile and play it on the tableau.  *)
local
  fun
    get' cd nil                  = raise Match             |
    get' (cd as {suit=_, value=13}) ((nil,nil)::rest)  =
      (cd::nil,nil)::rest                                  |
    get' cd ((x::y,z)::rest)  =
      if compat(cd,x)
        then (cd::x::y,z)::rest
        else (x::y,z)::(get' cd rest)                      |
    get' cd (p::rest)            = p::(get' cd rest)       ;
in
fun
  get {foundation=f, tableau=t, stock=(cd::r,left)} =
    {foundation=f, tableau=get' cd t, stock=(r,left)};
end;
```

The last possible play is to turn over a card from the stock to the discard pile.

```
(* Get another card from the stock.  *)
fun
  new {foundation=f, tableau=t, stock=(x,cd::r)} =
    {foundation=f, tableau=t, stock=(cd::x,r)};
```

The game proceeds by applying these moves until either the foundation is complete, or no move is possible. If no move is possible the game is lost. The following ML program continually applies the moves (in the order given subsequently) until the game is over. The function **play** returns true if the input deck of cards led to a winning game.

```
(*  Given a shuffled deck of cards, play a game of Klondike.  *)
local
  exception no_move of Layout;
  local
    fun
      apply nil    lay = raise no_move (lay) |
      apply (h::t) lay = h(lay) handle Match => apply t lay;
  in
    val move = apply [turn, stack, get, build, promote, new];
  end;
  fun loop (tab) : bool = win (tab) orelse (loop (move tab));
in
  fun play (deck: Card list) : bool =
    loop (init deck) handle no_move _ => false;
end;
```

It is possible to adjust the strategy of play by rearranging the order in which the function **apply** tries the moves. The possibilities, however, are limited. Some strategy is coded into the individual functions to implement the separate moves, and no mechanism is implemented to judge the relative merit of the different orders in which the individual moves could proceed.

Two important issues are illustrated by this example program: tail recursion and guards in patterns. We devote a couple of paragraphs now to point them out.

The function **play** was written using a subordinate function **loop**. This function tests each successive layout by calling itself recursively. Some may worry that such constructions should be avoided to minimize the number of costly procedure calls. In fact, this loop is every bit as efficient as a **while** loop in a conventional language. Any good implementation of the language will note that the recursive call by **loop** to itself does not warrant pushing another activation record on the run-time stack. Calls made at the end of the function—known as tail-recursive calls—can be treated in a special manner.

Because of the limitations of the language, we were coerced into a stratagem that was less than ideal. We implemented the moves of Klondike as functions that are applicable to the layout in certain patterns and that test the layout further for applicability, then make the move or raise an exception. One could hope that there would be a way to combine the test for applicabililty. ML patterns, however, can only distinguish structural differences, not test for equality of substructures or other semantic nuances. In the programming language Haskell patterns may have guards. The guards are arbitrary boolean expressions that may examine the substructures of the pattern. Thus, the outline of the **move** function would be clearer, and look something like the following:

```
fun
  move pat₁ | guard₁ = exp₁ |
  move pat₂ | guard₂ = exp₂ |
    ⋮
  move _ = raise Match;
```

■ Chapter 7

Types

To fully appreciate ML it is necessary to understand more about its unique type system. It is a tribute to the design of the language that programmers need to concern themselves so little with type checking. The process that the ML system uses to do type checking is important in its own right, however, and so we discuss a few of the basic principles in this chapter. Knowing more about polymorphism and type inference is also useful in interpreting the type errors that ML detects while compiling a program. In this chapter we describe the way type inferencing works in ML, the importance of the **let** statement in the type system, the interaction between overloading and type checking, and several other miscellaneous issues about types. The final two sections explain some of the theory behind defining the types of expressions and give a type-checking algorithm for a simplified version of ML.

7.1 MORE ABOUT POLYMORPHISM

Consider the following simple polymorphic function.

```
val f = (fn l => if null (l) then 0 else 1)
```

Computationally, the function **f** is not very interesting; we are interested in **f** for its structure. It has an **if** statement, an application of a function, and it is a function itself as evidenced by the keyword **fn**. We wish to consider the problem of determining the type of **f**.

We will determine the type of **f** making use of existing type information, for example, the type of **null**, and rules governing the type checking of constructs in the language, for example, the **if** statement. We assume that the following functions and constants have the indicated types.

```
null     : 'a list -> bool
0        : int
1        : int
```

Informally, we arrive at the conclusion that **f** has the type **'a list->int** as follows:

> The value **f** is a function, say it has type **'a -> 'b**, the return type must be the same as the type of the constant **0**, so **'b** is equal to **int**, and because **null** is applied to the argument **1**, which we have assumed has type **'a**, we must have **'a** is equal to **'c list**. Therefore the type of **f** must be **'c list -> int**, or equivalently **'a list -> int**.

More systematically we can view the type-checking rules of the language as requiring that certain expressions have certain types. For example, the type of a function definition must be an arrow type, say **'a -> 'b** for new, unencumbered type variables **'a** and **'b**.

```
(fn l => if null (l) then 0 else 1) : 'a -> 'b
```

Consequently, the formal argument **l** must have type **'a**, and the function body must have type **'b**. We set this down thus:

```
l                                         : 'a
if null(l) then 0 then 1                  : 'b
```

The function body is an **if** statement. The **if** statement requires the following three constraints.

```
null (l)                                  : bool
0                                         : 'b
1                                         : 'b
```

The only expression left to decompose is **null (l)**. The application of a function requires that the argument must have the type of the domain of the function. We are given that the type of the function **null** is **'a list -> bool**, which we rename to **'c list -> bool**. This is to keep the type separate from the use of the type variable **'a**, which was already chosen to stand for the type of the argument in the function definition.

```
l                                         : 'c list
```

Naturally, the same expression must have the same type throughout. So, for example, the identifier **1** has the same type everywhere it appears. Consequently, **'a** is equal to **'c list**. Also **'b** = **int**, as we were given that **0** and **1** have type **int**. So the question is: Can we find types for all the type variables we introduced that make all the type equations true simultaneously? If we can, then we know the expression is type correct—that is, no run-time type error can happen. Moreover, we have inferred the type of each expression. The programmer does not provide any type declarations. If we cannot find solutions, then the expression is not type correct. Unification is the name given to the process that finds types for type variables to make two polytypes equal. This process can be used to solve all the equations generated by the constraints. Unification is a well-studied problem, and there are good algorithms to solve it.

If the type checking requirements do not constrain the types of the expressions completely, some type variables will be left unspecified. This is how a polymorphic type is achieved. In the preceding example we have **'a** = **'c list** and **'b** = **int**. The type variable **'c** is unconstrained. We can substitute any type for **'c**, and the constraints issued earlier will still hold.

A complete description and proof of the constraint-generating approach to type checking can be found in [17]. Later in this chapter we develop a recursive algorithm for type checking.

In the previous example we have used the obvious rules for function definition, function application, and the conditional statement. Each construct of the language requires the appropriate constraints on the type of its pieces. These constraints are so few and so intuitive that we do not set down a comprehensive list. For example, it comes as no surprise that the type of tuple is the cartesian product of its constituent parts. We will remark, however, on two cases.

The first case is the **raise** construct. It is clear that the type of the expression raised with a **raise** statement must be of type **exn**, but what is the type of the **raise** statement, as in the following example?

```
ML> let
..>    exception e
..> in
..>    (fn 1 => if null (1) then 0 else raise e)
..> end;
```

The crux of the matter is that execution of a **raise** construct diverts the normal creation and manipulation of values until and unless an appropriate handler is found that continues creating and manipulating values. Because the value of the preceding function for non-null lists never exists, the compiler can assume whatever it likes about the expression **raise e**. It can assume that its type is `int`, so that the type of the preceding function becomes `'a list -> int`.

The second case concerns recursive function definitions. These definitions require an additional check. We consider the following simple case.

```
val rec f = (fn x => f (1,2))
```

The first obstacle in analyzing the function body is knowing what type the identifier `f` has. Since we initially know nothing about `f`, yet it is *not* an unbound variable, we give it the type `'e`, a type variable. The analysis of the function definition yields the following constraints:

```
(fn x => f (1,2)) : 'a -> 'b
             x : 'a
      (f (1,2)) : 'b
              f : 'c -> 'd
          (1,2) : 'c
      (f (1,2)) : 'd
              f : 'e
          (1,2) : int * int
```

We conclude that `'b='d`, `'c=int*int`, and `'e='c->'b=(int*int) ->'b`. Thus far we have not constrained `'a`, the type of the input to the function `f`. But recursive function definitions require that the type `'e` given to the function identifier must equal the type of the function definition, which, in this case, is `'a->'b`. From this additional constraint we conclude that `'a=int*int`.

The function `f` has an interesting type: `(int*int)->'a`. This type permits expressions like `tl(f(1,2))` and `if f(1,2) then 0 else 1`. At first one is tempted to conclude that the type system is failing to prevent a run-time type error. How can `f(1,2)` be both a list and a boolean value? However, the type system is sound—the execution of function `f` does not terminate for any input value, so we can assume anything we like about the return type.

7.2 MILNER `let` CONSTRUCT

The `let` construct is of vital importance to the type system in tne programming language ML. This is not at all obvious from the discussion of the language thus far. In this section we explain its key role in the type system.

Recall the syntax of the `let` statement:

```
let val id = exp1 in exp2 end
```

A moment's reflection convinces one that the expression is computationally equivalent to:

> **(fn** *id* **=>** *exp₂***)** **(***exp₁***)**

Consequently, one may be tempted to conclude that the **let** statement is not necessary at all, or perhaps that it is an insignificant syntactic convenience. This is far from that case, however. The **let** statement is *not* equivalent as far as type checking is concerned. In fact, it plays a crucial role in obtaining polymorphism.

Consider the following simple instance of the **let** statement:

```
ML> let val f = (fn x => x) in (f(2),f(true)) end;
    (2, true) : int * bool
```

The ML system successfully finds a type for this expression but fails to find a type for the following expression, which is computationally equivalent:

```
ML> (fn f => (f 2, f true)) (fn x => x)
Type error -- Cannot unify domain of function and its argument.
   The function:  f
   Domain of fun: int
   The argument:  true
   Type of arg:   bool
```

The **let** statement permits the type variable **'a** in **'a->'a**, the type of **(fn x=>x)**, to be instantiated differently each time required, once in **(f 2)** and again in **(f true)**.

It is not an option to conclude from *e* = **(fn f =>(f 2, f true))** that **f** has type **'a->'b**. If this were the type of **f**, then we should be able to apply the function *e* to the function **(fn n=>n+1)**, say, of type **int->int**. This would cause a run-time type error, however, when it was applied to **true**.

7.3 ILL-TYPED EXPRESSIONS

Not all syntactically correct expressions can be well-typed. These expressions usually are a result of the programmer using the variables in an inconsistent manner, and so it is useful that the ML system flags these problems.

In this example, the programmer is using **x** both as a function and as an argument to a function.

```
ML> fun f(x) = x x;
Type error -- Attempt to build a self-referential type.
The function:  x
Its argument:  x
```

This is mostly likely an error, but it could conceivably have been the intention of the programmer. The function **f** defined this way could reasonably be used with the identity function as an argument. Here is a hypothetical use of **f**.

```
f (fn x => x)
```

Although the previous use is reasonable,

```
f (sqrt);
```

is not. The ML type system is not sufficiently strong to distinguish the two cases, so the ML system must reject function definitions like **f**.

The error is detected because no type in the ML type system can be found for **x** which simultaneously satisfies the constraint that **x:'a->'b** and **x:'a**.

7.4 OVERLOADING

As a general design principle overloading has been avoided, as it does not interact well with the polymorphism in ML. However, the conventional use of the plus symbol to denote addition of integers and real numbers is quite natural, and ML permits this.

```
ML> 2+3;
    5 : int

ML> 2.0+3.0;
    5.0 : real
```

Overloading does interfere with the type inference process as shown in the next example.

```
ML> fun f (x,y) = x+y;
Semantic error -- Overloaded symbol "+" can't be resolved.
```

There is no way of knowing whether integer addition or real addition was meant. The ML system must know which instructions to generate for the addition. The universal polymorphism of ML is not a solution in this case as addition is defined for two particular types and is not defined uniformly for all types.

The standard [12] requires the presence in the initial environment of the usual operations on numbers **+**, **−**, *****, and the usual predicates **<**, **<=**, **>**, and **>=** to be defined on both integers and real numbers.

Cases of ambiguity, such as those illustrated in the last example, can be handled by explicitly indicating the type.

```
ML> fun f (x:int, y) = x+y;
    f = [function] : int * int -> int
```

The programmer may constrain the type of any expression in ML.   The syntax is *expr* : *type*. If the ML system finds *type* to be an instance of the type of *expr*, then it makes *expr* have type *type*.   Otherwise an error message is issued. This provides a way for the programmer to communicate the desired type. As we have seen, this is useful for overload resolution. It is also useful for documenting the program for the benefit of the human reader. It may also help localize type errors by asserting the programmer's belief about types of particular expressions.

7.5 EQUALITY AND IMPERATIVE TYPES

Equality acts like a polymorphic function of the type `'a * 'a -> bool`. It seems natural enough to apply the test of equality to all values *except* functions. What should be the result of the following comparison?

```
(fn x => x) = (fn x => x)
```

We could check if the two functions were syntactically equal (i.e., token for token equal) or generated the same code.   None of these interpretations is particularly useful, however. We could ask if the functions were extensionally equal—that is, if they computed the same results on corresponding input. But it is not possible to decide this problem in general. So we must prevent the application of equality on function types.

This poses a problem to the polymorphic type system. The standard [12] deals with this problem in a systematic way by requiring that each type variable be associated with a boolean attribute indicating whether or not the type admits equality. These type variables are distinguished from other type variables by beginning with two (not one) apostrophes.   Consider the following function definition:

```
ML> fun f x = if x=x then 1 else 0;
    val f = [function] : ''a -> int
```

the argument to the function **f** is immaterial as long as it admits equality. Thus **f** can be applied to integers but not functions. For example, **f 3** is legal, but **f (3,fn x=>x)** is not.

All types except **abstype** types and those containing a function type admit equality. Types defined by **abstype** do not admit equality, because the programmer may explicitly provide an equality operation, defined and named as desired. If one is not provided it is assumed that the intention was to omit it. This is important because many times there may be more than one representation of an abstract type. (Think of rational numbers represented by pairs of integers.) Then the system-provided equality may not be appropriate.

So equality does have a polymorphic type but to a limited extent.

```
ML> op =;
    val = [function] : ''a * ''a -> bool
```

The equality operation can be used as follows:

```
ML> map (op =) [(2,3), (1,1), (3,1)];
```

Imperative types are also distinguished. These types are necessary to overcome the challenge raised by polymorphic exceptions (see section 6.4.3) and by polymorphic references (see section 8.2). Although the specific types used by exceptions and references are not material, all uses must be consistent. This, too, conflicts with the polymorphism of ML which tries to permit polymorphic types to be instantiated differently in different contexts. Standard ML enforces a conservative regime in which imperative types are used when an exception or a reference could be generated.

Imperative type variables are those type variables beginning with one or two apostrophes followed by the underscore _ character.

7.6 COMPLEXITY

The complexity of deciding whether or not an expression has a type in ML is quite great, although this does not appear to be any problem in practice. It has been determined that the complexity of deciding whether or not an expression has a type in ML is exponentially hard [9]. The problem can be seen in the following example. Certain (artificially) constructed expressions may have very large types.

```
ML> let
..>    fun pair x y z = z x y;
..>    fun f1 y = pair y y;
..>    fun f2 y = f1 (f1 y);
..>    fun f3 y = f2 (f2 y);
..> in
..>    f3 (fn x => x)
..> end;
```

```
[function] : ((((((((('a -> 'a) -> ('a -> 'a) -> 'b) -> 'b) -> ((('a
-> 'a) -> ('a -> 'a) -> 'b) -> 'b) -> 'c) -> 'c) -> (((((('a -> 'a) ->
('a -> 'a) -> 'b) -> 'b) -> ((('a -> 'a) -> ('a -> 'a) -> 'b) -> 'b)
-> 'c) -> 'c) -> 'd) -> 'd) -> ((((((('a -> 'a) -> ('a -> 'a) -> 'b)
-> 'b) -> ((('a -> 'a) -> ('a -> 'a) -> 'b) -> 'b) -> 'c) -> 'c) ->
((((('a -> 'a) -> ('a -> 'a) -> 'b) -> 'b) -> ((('a -> 'a) -> ('a ->
'a) -> 'b) -> 'b) -> 'c) -> 'c) -> 'd) -> 'd) -> 'e) -> 'e
```

Because merely writing out a type whose length is so long when compared with the size of the program requires a long time, the whole type-checking process requires a long time in the worst case.

7.7 TYPING RULES

Sometimes it is important to define precisely what the type is of any expression in a polymorphic language. In the previous chapters the informal explanation serves as a useful guide, but no definitive explanation has been offered. In this section we describe how a formal definition relating expressions and types is possible, and we give the definition for a simple subset of the ML language. The complete details can be obtained from the language definition [12]. These same techniques are also used by the standard to define the dynamic semantics of the language using a Plotkin-style operational semantics.

We can consider the collections of types that an expression may assume as being defined by a formal proof system. A proof system is a highly structured means of representing a deduction by giving simple, mechanical steps. Each step yields a conclusion that can be used in the next step. All the steps together can be put into a proof tree that is a derivation of the appropriate conclusion. To give the proof system for types, we require two definitions.

One of the structures manipulated by the proof system for types is the type assignment. A *type assignment*, which we shall denote by the letter A, maintains the already established or given list of bindings of identifiers and their types. We can think of type assignments as represented by an association list. So, a particular assignment might be $A_0 = $ [("null",'a list -> bool)]. This assignment associates the identifier **null** with the type **'a list -> bool**.

A *typing judgment* is a triple of the form

$$A \vdash e : \tau$$

where A is a type assignment, e is an expression, and τ is a type. In this case, we say "expression e has type τ under the assignment A." We will use these typing judgments to define when an expression has a type. The next few paragraphs give a deductive system with which to derive typing judgments. If we can derive with this system that an expression has a type, then this type is one of the legal types for the expression. In this way the set of types for an expression is defined.

The type of an identifier x is determined by the context. For this reason a type assignment is necessary. If x has been bound by some **fn** construct, see the next rule, then x has some value in the assignment A. The value in A is the type of x. This is the content of the first rule in the deductive system.

$$\frac{}{A \vdash x \ : \ A(x)} \qquad \text{if } x \in \text{Dom}(A)$$

By this rule we mean: if x is one of the identifiers assigned a type by A, then the type of x is $A(x)$, the type associated to x by A; otherwise the rule does not apply.

The following rule is for function definitions:

$$\frac{A[x \mapsto \tau_1] \vdash e_1 \ : \ \tau_2}{A \vdash \ (\textbf{fn } x \Rightarrow e_1) \ : \ \tau_1 \ \text{->} \ \tau_2}$$

The type assignment denoted by $A[x \mapsto \tau_1]$ is just like the assignment A, except that the value for the variable x is the type τ_1. This rule is understood to mean that if we can derive that the type of the function body is τ_2 under the assumption that the formal parameter has type τ_1, then the type of the function is $\tau_1 \text{->} \tau_2$.

The following type rule is for the application of the expression e_1 to e_2.

$$\frac{A \vdash e_1 \ : \ \tau_1 \ \text{->} \ \tau_2, \qquad A \vdash e_2 \ : \ \tau_2}{A \vdash e_1 \ e_2 \ : \ \tau}$$

The type of the first expression e_1 must be a function. The type of the second expression must be equal to the domain of the type of e_1.

The following typing rule is for the conditional statement.

$$\frac{A \vdash e_1 \ : \ \textbf{bool}, \qquad A \vdash e_2 \ : \ \tau, \qquad A \vdash e_3 \ : \ \tau}{A \vdash \ (\textbf{if } e_1 \textbf{ then } e_2 \textbf{ else } e_3) \ : \ \tau}$$

Type checking can be viewed as proving theorems in the deductive system defined by the four preceding rules. Next we give an example of the derivation for the type of the expression $f = (\textbf{fn l=>if null l then 0 else 1})$. We require an initial environment or type assignment A_0 consisting of the types of the predefined function symbols. Let

$$A_0 = [("\textbf{null}", '\textbf{a list} \ \text{->} \ \textbf{bool}), ("\textbf{0}", \textbf{int}), ("\textbf{1}", \textbf{int})]$$

In the deduction we will use the rule for function definition, and this will require another assignment that we call A_1. The type assignment A_1 is just like A_0 except that the identifier **l** is associated with the type **'a list**. Thus,

A_1=[("l",'a list), ("null",'a list -> bool), ("0",int), ("1",int)]

The rule for function definition, the rule for function application, and the rule for the conditional statement are each used once. The rule that looks up an identifier in the type assignment is used four times.

$$\frac{\dfrac{A_1 \vdash \text{null}:\text{'a list->bool} \quad A_1 \vdash \text{1}:\text{'a list}}{A_1 \vdash \text{(null 1)}:\text{bool}} \qquad A_1 \vdash \text{0}:\text{int} \quad A_1 \vdash \text{1}:\text{int}}{\dfrac{A_1 \vdash \text{(if null 1 then 0 else 1)}:\text{int}}{A_0 \vdash \text{(fn 1 => if null 1 then 0 else 1)}:\text{'a list->int}}}$$

The conclusion is that the expression f has type **'a list->int**. It is possible to derive other types for f using other type assignments. Fortunately, there is one best type. This type is more general than all the other types capable of being derived for f. The others are all instances of the most general type. It is this type that the ML system declares to be "the" type of the expression.

7.8 TYPE-RECONSTRUCTION ALGORITHM

In this section we give an ML program **type_of** to find the most general type for an expression (in a simple subset of ML). This program completely subsumes the role of type checking. If the search for the most general type fails, then the expression does not have any type derivable from the deductive system given in the last section. Because this system is the definition of the type of an expression, the expression is not type correct.

If we gave the type of every function definition, as in

$$(\textbf{ fn } x : \tau \Rightarrow e)$$

type checking would be easy as every application of the rule for function definition would be entirely specified. Without hints of this form, the function **type_of** must do more work. In fact, it reconstructs the types of all variables introduced by the function definition construct. From these the types of all expressions are easily obtained.

The algorithm **type_of** is a theorem prover for the proof system for typings given in the last section. A crucial insight in designing a theorem prover lies in recognizing that unification can be used to force types to be the same. For example, the typing rule for function application requires the domain of the function to be the same as the type of the actual argument. If the domain is **'a list * bool** and the type of the argument is **unit list * 'b**, then mapping **'a** to **unit** and **'b** to **bool** makes the two identical. Such a mapping is called a *substitution*. The algorithm to find a substitution (if one exists) that makes two terms equal is called *unification*. Any substitution can be used to specialize a proof tree making the type of the conclusion an instance of the original type. Thus as long as two types are unifiable then appropriate proof trees can be found that result in the appropriate types being syntactically identical.

In this section we assume that we already have a unification function (this algorithm is given in section 9.3), and we give a program **type_of**, which uses it to find the type of simple ML expressions represented by the data structure **Expr** given earlier in section 5.4.

The data structure for type assignments is an association list.

```
type Assignment = (Variable, Type) Assoc;
```

We make use of the abstract data type for association lists defined earlier (section 5.3) with the functions **lookup** and **update**.

The function **type_of** determines the type of an expression. The function can fail if two types fail to unify or if the expression contains a free variable. In this case the exception **undefined** is raised.

```
exception undefined of Variable;

fun type_of(S:Substitution,A:Assignment,e:Expr): Substitution*Type =
  case e of
    Var v =>
      (S,value S (lookup(v,A))handle not_found=>raise undefined(v))|
    Num _ => (S, Int)      |
    Bln _ => (S, Bool)     |
    App (e1, e2) =>
      let
        val (S1,tau1) = type_of (S,A,e1);
        val (S2,tau2) = type_of (S1,A,e2);
        val new = new_variable ();
        val U = unify (tau1, Arrow (tau2, new), S2);
      in
        (U, value U new)
      end |
    Fun (v, e1) =>
      let
        val new = new_variable ();
        val (S1,tau1) = type_of (S, update(v,new,A), e1)
      in
        (S1, Arrow (value S1 new, tau1))
      end |
    Cond (e1,e2,e3) =>
      let
        val (S1,tau1) = type_of (S,A,e1);
        val U1 = unify (Bool, tau1, S1)
```

```
    val (S2,tau2) = type_of (U1,A,e2);
    val (S3,tau3) = type_of (S2,A,e3);
    val U2 = unify (value S3 tau2, tau3, S3)
  in
    (U2, value U2 tau3)
  end;
```

It is possible to prove that the type returned by **type_of** characterizés all the types derivable from the typing rules.   Any type derivable for the expression is an instance of the type returned by **type_of**. Thus, **type_of** can be used to determine if a typing $A \vdash e{:}\tau$ is derivable, by checking if τ is an instance of the type returned by **type_of** for e. If **type_of** fails, or τ is not an instance, then the typing is not derivable. Hence, **type_of** is a theorem prover for the proof system of typings.

■ Chapter 8

References and Streams

The portion of ML described thus far has been purely functional. All the ML expressions discussed return a value, and none of them causes any side effect. Programming in this way has certain advantages:

- The programmer can understand the programs easier, because every expression has the same value regardless of the context in which it appears.
- The programs can run faster, because the compiler can apply more optimizations.
- The order in which subexpressions are evaluated is less important, and opportunities exist to execute some code in parallel.

Occasionally, however, it is more efficient or more convenient to program by storing values in updatable locations, as in imperative languages. In this chapter we introduce some nonfunctional aspects of the language. In addition, the computer world that is external to the language can be viewed as an updatable object. In this chapter we introduce streams as a useful abstraction for defining the interface to the external world.

8.1 REFERENCE

It is possible to program in an imperative fashion, like in FORTRAN, Pascal or Ada, using variables and side effects. This can be integrated fairly smoothly into the language by adding a type constructor **ref** for references to objects.

```
ML> val x = ref 3;        (* Make x be a reference to 3.        *)
    val x = ref 3 : int.ref
```

The identifier **ref** is another type constructor in the language. Note that the data constructor likewise has the name **ref**. Thus **ref 3** is an anonymous reference to the value **3**, and **int ref** is the type of references to integers. We treat references like variables in conventional programming languages; we can assign new values to them with the assignment statement.

```
ML> x := 4;               (* Assign a new value to x.          *)
    () : unit
```

The assignment statement is a binary, infix function in ML.

```
ML> op :=;
    val := = [function] : 'a ref * 'a -> unit
```

The contents of a variable is denoted explicitly with a dereferencing function. This function is denoted by the symbolic identifier **!**.

```
ML> !;
    val ! = [function] : 'a ref -> 'a

ML> !x;                   (* What is x currently referring to? *)
    4 : int
```

For programmers accustomed to conventional languages it is strange at first to use an explicit dereferencing function. In most conventional languages this dereferencing is done implicitly by context—whether on the right-hand side of the assignment statement or not.

Sequencing is a new construct that is required when programming with side effects. In this style of programming, a subprogram is often designed to cause several side effects one after another. For example, in the previous chapter we made use of a function that generates new variables names. This function called **new** makes use of sequencing. The basic idea is to keep an internal counter, and every time a function is called, increment the counter and form a string based on the value of the counter. The following declaration defines two functions **reset** and **new**.

```
ML> local
..>    val counter = ref 0;
..> in
..>    fun reset () = (counter := 0);
..>    fun new () =
```

```
..>        (counter := (!counter) + 1; "$" ^ makestring(!counter)));
..> end;
    val reset = [function] : unit -> unit;
    val new   = [function] : unit -> bool;
```

The function **reset** has an argument (all functions must have arguments). Since the argument is not important it takes an argument of type **unit**. Thus a type correct application of this function implies that the argument is the unit value **()**. So the function gets the one and only argument it expects. The function assigns zero to the local variable **counter** each time it is called. The function **new** also takes an argument of type **unit**. It generates the strings **"$1"**, **"$2"**, and so on. Because of the local declaration, the variable **counter** is not visible outside the declaration. This protects the contents of the variable from tampering by all means other than through the functions **reset** and **new**. Note that the value binding

```
ML> val reset = (counter := 0);      (*  Not useful  *)
    val reset = () : unit
```

permanently makes the value of **reset** to be **()**, and accessing the value

```
ML> reset;
    () : unit
```

causes no side effect. To cause a side effect on demand in the future, a *function* must be defined.

Like the function **reset**, the function **new** is a function with domain **unit**. Also like the function **reset**, it causes a side effect every time it is called. The function **new**, however, returns a value—a different one every time for as long as the counter is not reset. So to accomplish both an assignment and to return a value, the function **new** uses a construct of the form:

$$(exp \; ; \; \ldots \; ; \; exp)$$

The parentheses are a necessary part of the syntax. The expressions are all evaluated (for their side effects presumably) in order, one by one; then the value of the last expression is returned. This is how a sequence of side effects can be executed in ML. Notice that the syntax is similar to that of tuples,

```
ML> (reset (); 5; new (); new (); (1,2,3));
    (1,2,3) : int * int * int
```

For convenience it is possible to write

$$\mathbf{let} \; \cdots \; \mathbf{in} \; exp \; ; \; \ldots \; ; \; exp \; \mathbf{end}$$

for

```
let ··· in (exp ; ... ; exp) end
```

thereby sparing the parentheses in a **let** construct. The same convention does not apply to the **local** construct, as the body of a **local** construct consists of declarations (separated by optional semicolons), not expressions.

We make one final note about the form of sequencing in ML. Often it is convenient to obtain the sequential execution of expressions that have side effects by using the **let** construct.

```
let
    val _ = exp;
    val _ = exp;
    ⋮
in
    ...
end
```

This approach integrates well with the usual use of the **let** construct in programs without side effects.

A simple example of sequencing is the imperative analog of the function **map**. The function **map** applies a polymorphic function **f:'a->'b** to every member of an **'a list**. The function **app** also applies a polymorphic function **f:'a->'b** to every member of an **'a list** but throws the result of each application away. Presumably **f** is applied for the sake of some side effect; perhaps **'b** is equal to **unit**. Here is the definition of **app**.

```
ML> fun
..>   app f (nil) = ()          |
..>   app f (h::t) = (f h; app f t);   (* Do f to h; then do f to rest. *)
    val app = [function] : ('a -> 'b) -> 'a list -> unit
```

Another example use of sequencing are "memo" functions.   A memo function remembers the values that have been previously computed and avoids recomputing them. The first time the function is called for some input value, it must compute the result from scratch; thereafter, the function consults its memory. We can write an ML higher-order function that takes a function **f** as input and returns the so-called memoized version. The function **memoize** makes use of the abstract type **('a,'b)Assoc** defined earlier (in section 5.3) to remember pairs of input-output values computed previously.

```
fun memoize f =
    let
```

```
   val table = ref empty;        (* polymorphic association list *)
   fun g (x) =
     lookup (x, !table) handle not_found =>
       let
         val y = f x;
       in
         (table := update (x, y, !table); y)
       end
in
   g                             (* g is memoized version of f    *)
end;
```

Each memoized function must have its own private table of remembered pairs—hence, the structure

```
fun memoize f =
  let
   val table = · · ·
   ⋮
```

Conversely, the structure

```
local
  val table = · · ·
in
  fun memoize f =
    ⋮
```

would create one global and shared table for all the memoized functions. This would be incorrect.

The ML language has a **while** construct that makes it possible to program much like in conventional languages. Here is an example of a **while** statement used to decrement a reference to an integer.

```
ML> val n = ref 7;
    val n = ref 7 : int ref

ML> while !n>0 do n := !n -1 ;
    () : unit
```

The general form of the **while** construct is

> while exp_1 do exp_2

and the type of the construct is **unit**. The execution of the **while** statement has the usual semantics: the condition is evaluated; if true, then the second expression is evaluated. This is repeated until the condition evaluates to false. Presumably exp_2 has some side effect. Also, it usually executes more than one expression in sequence. The condition is most likely *not* an expression that yields the same (boolean) value each time it is evaluated. Here is a typical example.

```
ML> val sum = ref 0;
    val sum = ref 0 : int ref

ML> (n := 0; sum := 0; while !n<10 do (sum := !sum + !n; n := !n+1));
    () : unit

ML> !sum;
    45 : int
```

The **while** construct can be defined in terms of sequencing and recursion. The following is how the semantics of **while** exp_1 **do** exp_2 is defined:

```
let
  val rec f = fn () => if exp₁ then (exp₂; f()) else ()
in
  f()
end
```

A recursive auxiliary function with argument of type **unit** is defined to test the condition of the loop, exp_1, and execute the body, exp_2. The result of executing exp_2 is thrown away, and the function calls itself. A good compiler can compile such functions in a manner that avoids the overhead of repeated subprogram invocation. This is another example of tail recursion.

8.2 PROBLEMS WITH REFERENCES

Earlier (section 6.4.3) we gave an example illustrating the problem with values raised with exceptions whose types are polytypes. References have the same problem. References, like exceptions, act like a channel of information. Objects can be put in and taken out. The channel itself does not care what type the objects have, but the language must enforce that the objects actually removed from the channel are of a type expected.

The following simple example illustrates the problem with references. First we give a typical polymorphic use of a function bound using the **let** construct.

```
ML> let val f = (fn x=>x) in (f [1,2], f "a") end;
    ([1,2], "a") : int list * string
```

The function **f** can be safely used on lists of integers and on strings. If we use
the **let** statement to bind **f** to a reference to a function, the situation changes.

```
ML> let val f = ref (fn x => x)
..> in
..>    (f := (fn x => 3); if ((!f) "s") then 2 else 3)
..> end;
Semantic error -- Reference must be constrained by monotype.
```

8.3 STREAMS

A *stream* is a sequence of data elements of indefinite length accessible one by
one as each becomes available or is produced. A stream of characters is a
reasonable way to view a file. Consequently, accessing files in ML is centered
around streams.

open_in	**string -> instream**	uses the string as a file name to open for reading
open_out	**string -> outstream**	uses the string as a file name to open for writing; creates the file if necessary
input	**instream*int->string**	removes some number of characters from an input stream when available
output	**outstream*string->unit**	writes the string to the output stream
lookahead	**instream -> string**	returns the next character from an input stream when available without taking it out of the stream
close_out	**outstream -> unit**	closes an output stream
close_in	**instream -> unit**	closes an input stream
end_of_stream	**instream -> bool**	tests if there are any more characters left in an input stream
std_in	**instream**	a stream corresponding to the usual input device
std_out	**outstream**	a stream corresponding to the usual output device

The implementation of these functions is fairly closely tied with the UNIX operating system; however, in principle, they can be implemented in other environments as well.

The ML language has two built-in data types for stream objects. They are called **instream** and **outstream**. An **instream** is a place from which to receive characters. The predefined constant **std_in** is an **instream** that usually corresponds to the characters coming from the normal input device. An **outstream** is a place to which to send characters. The predefined constant **std_out** is an **outstream** that usually corresponds to the normal output device.

The table on page 136 gives the functions on streams that Standard ML requires. The function **input** (s, n) reads n characters from the input stream s. If the n characters are available it removes them from the stream and returns a string made of the characters. If there are fewer than n characters left in the stream, a string of the remaining characters is returned. Otherwise the function waits until the characters are produced. In certain circumstances the function **input** and the function **output** may raise the exception **Io**.

8.4 DIRECTIVES

We have already seen some directives. We have seen the **infix** and the **infixr** directives that alert the parser to the special syntax of some identifiers. In addition, there is the **nonfix** directive that revokes the infix status of an identifier.

> **infix** d id_1, $\ldots$ id_n binary, left associative
> **infixr** d id_1, $\ldots$ id_n binary, right associative
> **noninfix** id_1, $\ldots$ id_n not infix

The decimal digit d is optional and defaults to 0. The higher the value of this digit, the tighter the operator binds.

Only value identifiers (not types or labels) can be written infix. These directives are not an integral part of the mechanism that binds identifiers. The infix status belongs to the name until it is canceled, not to the binding. So it is wise to avoid using the same name with different infix status. The definition of Standard ML permits the use of these three directives inside **let** and **local** constructs, which limits the effect of the directive to the body of the construct.

Another important directive is the **use** command, which directs that the input be taken from another file. This is not part of the definition of Standard ML but is present in SML of NJ, for instance. This is useful for taking input from a file during an interactive session. The syntax is simple.

> **use** *"filename"*

8.5 EXAMPLE PROGRAM: STRIP

We end this chapter with an example ML program that makes use of the features described in this chapter. The program is called **strip**; it reads input from an external file line by line and writes out portions of some of the lines.

An important auxiliary function is **input_line**. This recursive function reads in the input a line at a time.

```
(* read a line from an instream *)
fun input_line ins =
 let
   val s = input (ins, 1);   (*  read one character, if available  *)
 in
   if s="" orelse s="\n" then s else s ^ (input_line ins)
 end;
```

The function **input_line** accumulates the line, character by character; the function calls itself recursively until the newline character or the end-of-file condition (**s=""**) is reached.

The function **strip** takes as input a string—the name of a TEX file. It reads the file and throws away all lines that do not begin with the prompt of the ML system. The remaining lines, minus the prompt, are written to the output. The name of the output file is derived from the input file by adding the suffix **"-strip.sml"**. The output file is presumably suitable for input to the ML system.

```
nonfix o;   (*  o (function composition) is pre-defined infix  *)

local
  val prompt  = "ML> " and prompt' = "..> ";
  val n  = size prompt and n' = size prompt';

  (*  Cause resulting ML program to write a separating comment.  *)
  fun sep (n: int) =
    let
      val c =  "(*  phrase " ^ (makestring n) ^ "  *)";
    in
      c ^ " val _ = output (std_out, \"" ^ c ^ "\\n\");\n"
    end;

  val count = ref 0;     (*  keep track of the number of phrases  *)

  fun first (o,s) =
    (count := !count + 1; output (o, sep (!count)); output (o, s));
```

```
fun each_line (o,line) =
  if (substring (line, 0, n) = prompt) handle Substring => false
    then first (o, substring (line, n, (size line)-n))
    else if (substring(line,0,n')=prompt') handle Substring=>false
      then output (o, substring (line, n', (size line)-n'))
      else ();

fun f (i,o) =
  while not (end_of_stream i) do each_line (o, input_line i);
in
  fun strip (file: string) =
    let
      val ins = open_in (file ^ ".tex");
      val outs = open_out (file ^ "-strip.sml");
      val _ = count := 0;
      val _ = f (ins, outs) handle _ => ();
      val _ = close_in ins;
      val _ = close_out outs;
    in
      ()
    end;
end;
```

The functions **makestring** and **substring** are left as exercises.

The function **strip** could be (and was) used to strip the ML programs out of the chapters of this book using the following ML expression:

```
app strip ["basic", "valb", "fun", "exc", "user", "type", "ref"]
```

Chapter 9

Structures

The **signature** and **structure** constructs are the mechanisms provided by ML to aggregate functions, types, and exceptions into meaningful units that can be manipulated as wholes. Such facility is necessary for any language to be used with serious programming. For instance, the absence of any sort of module construct plagues programming in the language C and helps propel the use of C++. The absence of modules made Pascal less effective too, spurring the need for the Modula family of languages.

9.1 SIGNATURE AND STRUCTURES

A module consists of two parts: a signature and a structure. A signature is a specification of a collection of declarations. A structure provides the implementation. We give an example for a module for rational numbers.

The following signature announces that rational numbers consist of a data type called **Rational** and three operations.

```
signature RationalNumbersSig =
  sig
    type Rational
    val Eq: Rational * Rational -> bool
    val Add: Rational * Rational -> Rational
    val Mult: Rational * Rational -> Rational
  end
```

The name of the signature is **RationalNumbersSig**.

An implementation of the preceding signature is given by the following structure named **RationalNumbers.**

```
structure RationalNumbers : RationalNumbersSig =
  struct
    type Rational = {Numerator: int, Denominator: int}
    fun Num ({Numerator=x, Denominator=_}:Rational) = x
    fun Den ({Numerator=_, Denominator=x}:Rational) = x

    fun Eq (x,y) = (Num(x)*Den(y) = Num(y)*Den(x))

    fun Add (x,y): Rational =
      {Numerator  = Num(x)*Den(y)+Num(y)*Den(x),
       Denominator= Den(x)*Den(y)}

    fun Mult (x,y): Rational =
      {Numerator=Num(x)*Num(y), Denominator = Den(x)*Den(y)}
  end
```

The functions **Num** and **Den** are used in the implementation of the rational numbers, but are not part of the signature.

The "dot" notation is used to access members of signatures.

```
RationalNumbers.Mult
    ({Numerator=3, Denominator=4}, {Numerator=1, Denominator=4})
```

The entire structure can be accessed without the "dot" notation using the **open** directive:

```
open <structure name>
```

Of course, this will hide the names of any identifier provided by the structure which have been previously declared.

9.2 FUNCTORS

In the modular construction of programs it is likely that a structure depends on functions and types from other parts of the program. It is desirable to isolate a structure as much as possible from these dependencies. It is also desirable to make these dependencies explicit. In terms of program constructs, we want to make a structure dependent on the identifiers that occur without definition in the structure. For example,

```
type X = real * int;
fun g (n) = 8*n;

structure Example =
  struct
    datatype T = con1 of int | con2 of X
    fun f (x) = con1 (x+g(2))
  end;
```

The free identifiers in the structure **Example** are the types **X** and **int** and the functions **+** and **g**. Now we may find **int** and **+** so unproblematic that we may choose to ignore them. The other identifiers we can collect into a structure and signature of their own.

```
signature DependSig =
  sig
    type X;
    val g : int -> int;
  end;

structure Depend : DependSig =
  struct
    type X = real * int;
    fun g (n) = 8*n;
  end;
```

The structure **Example** would be better understood as a function of **DependSig**—a function that produces a structure.

Structure-producing functions exist in Standard ML and are called *functors*. The functor appropriate for the preceding example is as follows:

```
functor ExampleFun (D: DependSig) =
  struct
    datatype T = con1 of int | con2 of D.X
    fun f(x) = con1 (x+D.g(2))
  end;
```

Notice the use of the dot notation to access members of the formal structure parameter **D**. Functor application is necessary to create the structure.

```
structure Example = ExampleFun (Depend);
```

This structure is like the previous **Example** structure. It is created using the functor **ExampleFun** applied to the structure **Depend** and not by explicitly listing the elements between the keywords **struct** and **end**.

9.3 EXAMPLE PROGRAM: UNIFICATION

In this section we demonstrate the use of structures, signatures, and functors on a nontrivial application. We design a general unification algorithm using a functor. The input structure describes the system of terms to unify, and the output structure provides a unification algorithm.

We begin by specifying a data structure **TT** that captures the common structure of terms required by unification. This structure divides terms into variables and operators applied to other terms. The data type **Term** is the user-provided data structure of terms; these are the terms we wish to unify. The functions **convert** and **unconvert** translate between the type **Term** and **TT**. These functions reveal how the type **Term** is to be understood by the unification algorithm. All these components are specified in the signature **TERMS**.

```
signature TERMS =
  sig
    eqtype Operator and Variable and Term;
    datatype TT = TO of Operator * TT list | TV of Variable;
    val convert   : Term -> TT;
    val unconvert : TT -> Term;
  end;
```

We need to assume that we can test operators, variables, and terms for equality. Hence, the types representing them are specified as **eqtype** types in Standard ML.

The unification functor promises to deliver a unification algorithm **unify**. Actually, this function is not self-contained as the output is a substitution. We must consider how best to deal with substitutions. We choose to specify the type **Substitution** as well as ancillary functions **id**, for the identity substitution, and **value**, which applies a substitution to a term. One other design choice is visible in the signature of **UNIFICATION**. The function **unify** takes a substitution as one of its three arguments. This generalization is slightly more convenient when using unification in the type-reconstruction algorithm **type_of** we did earlier (see section 7.8).

```
signature UNIFICATION =
  sig
    type Term and Substitution;
    exception non_unifiable and occurs_check;
    val unify : (Term * Term * Substitution) -> Substitution;
    val id    : Substitution;
    val value : Substitution -> Term -> Term;
  end;
```

The functor **Unification** takes a structure for terms and provides the function **unify**.

```
functor Unification (Terms: TERMS) : UNIFICATION =
  struct
    type Term = Terms.Term;

    type Substitution = Terms.Variable -> Terms.Term;

    val id = (Terms.unconvert o Terms.TV);

    fun upd (v: Terms.Variable, t) (S) (v1:Terms.Variable) =
      if v=v1 then t else (S v1);

    fun
      top S (Terms.TV v) = S v   |
      top S (x)          = x     ;

    fun
      value' S (Terms.TV v)       = S v                             |
      value' S (Terms.TO(O,args)) = Terms.TO(O, map (value' S) args);

    fun value (S: Substitution) t : Terms.Term =
      Terms.unconvert (value' (Terms.convert o S) (Terms.convert t));

    exception non_unifiable and occurs_check and length;
    fun
      pairup (nil, nil)   = nil                         |
      pairup (a::b, c::d) = (a,c)::(pairup (b,d)) |
      pairup (_)          = raise length;

    fun
      occurs v (Terms.TV w)        = (v = w)   |
      occurs v (Terms.TO (O, args)) = exists (occurs v) args;

    fun
      subst(t,v)(Terms.TV w)       = if v=w then t else (Terms.TV w) |
      subst(t,v)(Terms.TO(O,args))=Terms.TO(O,map (subst(t,v)) args);

    fun unify' ((t1,t2),S) =
      let
        val t1' = top S t1 and t2' = top S t2;
      in
        case (t1', t2') of
          (Terms.TV v,Terms.TV w)=>if (v=w) then S else upd(v,t2')S |
          (Terms.TV v, _)            =>
            if occurs v t2 then raise occurs_check else upd(v,t2')S |
```

```
        (_, Terms.TV w)           =>
          if occurs w t1 then raise occurs_check else upd(w,t1')S |
        (Terms.TO (o1, tlist1), Terms.TO (o2, tlist2)) =>
          if o1=o2
            then fold unify' (pairup (tlist1, tlist2)) S
            else raise non_unifiable
      end;

  fun unify (t1,t2,S) =
    let
      val t = (Terms.convert t1, Terms.convert t2)
    in
      Terms.unconvert o unify'(t, Terms.convert o S)
    end;
  end;
```

Having defined the functor **Unification**, we now apply it to the type terms for the simple ML-like language introduced earlier.

```
type TypeVariable = string;
datatype Type =
  TypeVar of TypeVariable |
  Bool                    |
  Int                     |
  Arrow of Type * Type    ;
```

These type terms can be viewed as variables and three type operators. The type operations **Bool** and **Int** are 0-ary operators or constants. **Arrow** is a binary operator. This is evident in the definition of **convert** and **unconvert** given in the next structure. To use the unification function we must first apply the **Unification** functor to a structure with signature **TERMS**. This puts the data type **Type** in a form suitable for unification. The structure, which we call **Terms**, is as follows:

```
structure Terms : TERMS =
  struct
    datatype Operator = bool | int | arrow | list;
    type Variable = TypeVariable;
    type Term  = Type;
    datatype TT = TO of Operator * TT list | TV of Variable;
    fun
      convert (TypeVar v) = (TV v)                                   |
      convert (Bool)      = TO (bool, nil)                           |
      convert (Int)       = TO (int, nil)                            |
      convert (Arrow(d,r))= TO (arrow,(convert d)::(convert r)::nil);
```

```
    exception bad_rep of Operator;
    fun
      unconvert(TV v)                 = (TypeVar v)
      unconvert(TO (bool, nil))       = Bool
      unconvert(TO (int, nil))        = Int
      unconvert(TO(arrow,d::r::nil))= Arrow(unconvert d,unconvert r)
      unconvert(TO (oper, args))      = raise bad_rep (oper)
  end;
```

All that remains to be done to obtain the function to unify types is to apply the functor **Unification** to the structure **Terms**. This is done subsequently, and we name the resulting structure **Unify**.

```
structure Unify = Unification (Terms);
```

The structure **Unify** has the signature **UNIFICATION**, which means we have made available a function **unify**, a type **Substitution**, and so on. For example, the expression

```
Unify.unify (TypeVar "alpha", Arrow (Bool, TypeVar "beta"), Unify.id)
```

results in the substitution mapping **"alpha"** to the arrow type. The expression

```
Unify.unify (Bool, Int, Unify.id)
```

results in the exception **non_unifiable**. The expression

```
Unify.unify
  (TypeVar "alpha", Arrow(TypeVar "alpha",TypeVar "beta"), Unify.id)
```

results in the exception **occurs_check**.

SML of NJ

Every implementation of ML provides an environment of predefined functions. For reference we give the signatures that comprise the predefined data structures and functions available in SML of NJ:

```
(* Copyright 1989 by AT&T Bell Laboratories *)
signature REF =
  sig
    infix 3 :=
    val ! : 'a ref -> 'a
    val := : 'a ref * 'a -> unit
    val inc : int ref -> unit
    val dec : int ref -> unit
  end

signature LIST =
  sig
    infixr 5 :: @
    datatype 'a list = :: of ('a * 'a list) | nil
    exception Hd
    exception Tl
    exception Nth
    exception NthTail
    val hd : 'a list -> 'a
    val tl : 'a list -> 'a list
    val null : 'a list -> bool
    val length : 'a list -> int
    val @ : 'a list * 'a list -> 'a list
    val rev : 'a list -> 'a list
```

```
      val map :  ('a -> 'b) -> 'a list -> 'b list
      val fold : (('a * 'b) -> 'b) -> 'a list -> 'b -> 'b
      val revfold : (('a * 'b) -> 'b) -> 'a list -> 'b -> 'b
      val app : ('a -> 'b) -> 'a list -> unit
      val revapp : ('a -> 'b) -> 'a list -> unit
      val nth : 'a list * int -> 'a
      val nthtail : 'a list * int -> 'a list
      val exists : ('a -> bool) -> 'a list -> bool
    end

signature ARRAY =
  sig
    infix 3 sub
    type 'a array
    exception Subscript
    val array : int * '1a -> '1a array
    val sub : 'a array * int -> 'a
    val update : 'a array * int * 'a -> unit
    val length : 'a array -> int
    val arrayoflist : '1a list -> '1a array
  end

signature BYTEARRAY =
  sig
    infix 3 sub
    eqtype bytearray
    exception Subscript
    exception Range
    val array : int * int -> bytearray
    val sub : bytearray * int -> int
    val update : bytearray * int * int -> unit
    val length : bytearray -> int
    val extract : bytearray * int * int -> string
    val fold : ((int * 'b) -> 'b) -> bytearray -> 'b -> 'b
    val revfold : ((int * 'b) -> 'b) -> bytearray -> 'b -> 'b
    val app : (int -> 'a) -> bytearray -> unit
    val revapp : (int -> 'b) -> bytearray -> unit
  end

signature IO =
  sig
    type instream
    type outstream
    exception Io of string
    val std_in : instream
    val std_out : outstream
    val std_err : outstream
    val open_in : string -> instream
```

```
      val open_out : string -> outstream
      val open_append : string -> outstream
      val open_string : string -> instream
      val close_in : instream -> unit
      val close_out : outstream -> unit
      val output : outstream * string -> unit
      val outputc : outstream -> string -> unit
      val input : instream * int -> string
      val inputc : instream -> int -> string
      val input_line : instream -> string
      val lookahead : instream -> string
      val end_of_stream : instream -> bool
      val can_input : instream -> int
      val flush_out : outstream -> unit
      val is_term_in : instream -> bool
      val is_term_out : outstream -> bool
      val set_term_in : instream * bool -> unit
      val set_term_out : outstream * bool -> unit
      val execute : string -> instream * outstream
      val exportML : string -> bool
      val exportFn : string * (string list*string list->unit) -> unit
      val use : string -> unit
      val use_stream : instream -> unit
    end


signature BOOL =
  sig
    datatype bool = true | false
    datatype 'a option = NONE | SOME of 'a   (* stuck in here for
                                                   convenience *)
    val not : bool -> bool
    val print : bool -> unit
    val makestring : bool -> string
  end


signature STRING =
  sig
    infix 6 ^
    infix 4 > < >= <=
    type string
    exception Substring
    val length : string -> int
    val size : string -> int
    val substring : string * int * int -> string
    val explode : string -> string list
    val implode : string list -> string
    val <= : string * string -> bool
```

```
      val <  : string * string -> bool
      val >= : string * string -> bool
      val >  : string * string -> bool
      val ^  : string * string -> string
      exception Chr
      val chr : int -> string
      exception Ord
      val ord : string -> int
      val ordof : string * int -> int
      val print : string -> unit
    end


signature INTEGER =
  sig
    infix 7 * div mod quot rem
    infix 6 + -
    infix 4 > < >= <=
    exception Sum and Diff and Prod and Neg
    exception Div and Mod
    exception Overflow
    type int
    val ~ : int -> int
    val * : int * int -> int
    val div : int * int -> int
    val mod : int * int -> int
    val quot : int * int -> int
    val rem : int * int -> int
    val + : int * int -> int
    val - : int * int -> int
    val >  : int * int -> bool
    val >= : int * int -> bool
    val <  : int * int -> bool
    val <= : int * int -> bool
    val min : int * int -> int
    val max : int * int -> int
    val abs : int -> int
    val print : int -> unit
    val makestring : int -> string
  end


signature BITS =
  sig
    type int
    val orb : int * int -> int
    val andb : int * int -> int
    val xorb : int * int -> int
    val lshift : int * int -> int
```

```
    val rshift : int * int -> int
    val notb : int * int -> int
  end


signature REAL =
  sig
    infix 7 * /
    infix 6 + -
    infix 4 > < >= <=
    type real
    exception Sum and Diff and Prod
    exception Floor and Sqrt and Exp and Ln
    exception Div
    exception Overflow
    val ~ : real -> real
    val + : (real * real) -> real
    val - : (real * real) -> real
    val * : (real * real) -> real
    val / : (real * real) -> real
    val > : (real * real) -> bool
    val < : (real * real) -> bool
    val >= : (real * real) -> bool
    val <= : (real * real) -> bool
    val abs : real ->  real
    val real : int -> real
    val floor : real -> int
    val truncate : real -> int
    val ceiling : real -> int
    val sqrt : real -> real
    val sin : real -> real
    val cos : real -> real
    val arctan : real -> real
    val exp : real -> real
    val ln : real -> real
    val print : real -> unit
    val makestring : real -> string
  end


signature GENERAL =
  sig
    infix 3 o
    infix before
    exception Bind
    exception Match
    exception Interrupt
(* NOTE: Interrupt is never raised by the system, but is
 * included to provide some compatibility with the definition. *)
```

```
type 'a cont
val callcc : ('a cont -> 'a) -> 'a
val throw : 'a cont -> 'a -> 'b

val o : ('b -> 'c) * ('a -> 'b) -> ('a -> 'c)
val before : ('a * 'b) -> 'a

type exn
type unit
infix 4 = <>
val = : ''a * ''a -> bool
val <> : ''a * ''a -> bool
end
```

Exercises

1. Give the type of the following ML expression:
   ```
   [ ( [1, 2], ("a", true) ), ( [], ("ab", false) ) ]
   ```

2. Write a binary function that returns both the integer quotient and remainder of the input.

3. Write a single pattern that does not exhaust all possible values of type **int*int**.

4. Write a function **append** to append two lists together (without using the built-in function @ to do so). Use **append** to write a function that reverses the elements of a list.

5. How many total calls to the function **::** are made in computing the reverse of a list of length *n* using the function requested in the previous exercise? Write another function that reverses the elements of a list that does not use append and requires only *n* calls to the function **::** for a list of length *n*.

6. Write a function **pairup** that takes two lists of equal length as arguments and returns a single list. This list consists of pairs, the first element from the first input list and the second element from the second list.

7. Write a function **makestring** that takes an integer and returns the decimal representation as a string of characters.

   ```
   ML> makestring (23-57);
       "~34" : string
   ```

8. Write a function **substring (s: string, index: int, len: int)** that extracts the substring of **s** with length **len** beginning at position **index** (let the first position be 0). If the position or the length is negative, or in any other way not appropriate for the string **s**, the function should raise the exception **Substring**.

9. Write a function to sort a list of integers.

10. Write a function **curry3** to curry a function of three arguments. The function should have the following type:

```
('a * 'b * 'c -> 'd) -> 'a -> 'b -> 'c -> 'd
```

11. Write a function **uncurry** that takes a higher-order function and returns a binary function. The function should have the following type:

```
('a -> 'b -> 'c) -> 'a * 'b -> 'c
```

12. Write a function **F** that composes an input function n times with itself. Formally we want

$$\mathbf{F}(0)(f)(x) = x$$

$$\mathbf{F}(n)(f)(x) = \underbrace{f(\cdots(f(x))\cdots)}_{n}$$

The function should begin as follows and use an **if** statement:

```
fun F (n: int) (f: 'a->'a) (x: 'a) =
```

Now write the same function using function definition by case analysis.

13. Write a function that increments the **m** field of a record with type **{l:int,m:int, n:int}**. The function should return a record of the same type.

14. Why is it not possible to write a polymorphic function to increment just one field, say **m**, of a record that works for any record containing the field **m**? The function should return a record of the same type as the input.

15. Write a function **f** *without* using exceptions that has type **(int*real)->'a**. What is the result of **f(1,4.3)**?

16. Using the following data structure for binary trees

```
datatype Tree = empty | node of int * Tree * Tree;
```

accumulate all the integers in a tree in depth-first order.

17. Accumulate all the integers in breadth-first order for a binary tree as defined in the previous exercise.

18. Design a concrete data type for regular expressions. Here is a BNF description of a syntax for regular expressions.

<rexp> ::= *<character>*	character matches itself
<rexp> ::= .	matches anything
<rexp> ::= *<rexp>* *<rexp>*	concatenation
<rexp> ::= *<rexp>* *	0, 1 or more times
<rexp> ::= *<rexp>* +	1 or more times

$\langle rexp \rangle ::= \langle rexp \rangle$?	optional (0 or 1 times)
$\langle rexp \rangle ::= (\langle rexp \rangle)$	parenthesization
$\langle rexp \rangle ::= $ "$\langle metacharacter \rangle$	escape metacharacters

The syntactic category of $\langle character \rangle$ includes all the ASCII characters except the metacharacters `. * + ? ( ) \`.

19. Use the data type for regular expressions in the previous exercise to write a boolean function **match** that checks if a string is among the strings generated by a regular expression. The function should begin as follows:

```
fun match (r: Rexp) (s: string) : bool =
```

20. Write a function that parses strings into the data type for regular expressions created for exercise 18.

21. Design an abstract data type for stacks. There should be operations for creating, popping, and pushing an element in the stack, as well as a test for the empty stack.

22. Design a data structure for an association list with integer keys using some hashing technique.

23. What language facilities would be necessary to implement an association list with hashing for keys of any arbitrary types?

24. Design a data structure for a labeled, directed graph. Write a topological sort function for graphs. The output should be a list of labels such that if there is a directed path from vertex v_1 to v_2, then the label for vertex v_1 must precede the label for vertex v_2 in the list. If there is no such ordering, the function should raise an exception.

25. Write a purely functional program that solves the following puzzle invented by John Conway. The puzzle is to build an entire $5 \times 5 \times 5$ cube out of eighteen pieces of four different rectangular solids. The pieces can be placed in any orientation.

Number of Pieces	Size of Piece
13	$1 \times 2 \times 4$
3	$1 \times 1 \times 3$
1	$2 \times 2 \times 2$
1	$1 \times 2 \times 2$

26. Show how the type of the following ML function is inferred

```
fun map (f,l) =
  if null(l) then nil else cons (f (hd l), map (f, tl l));
```

given the types of the following identifiers:

```
null : 'a list -> bool
 nil : 'a list
cons : 'a * 'a list -> 'a list
  hd : 'a list -> 'a
  tl : 'a list -> 'a list
```

27. Give the most general type (if it exists) of the following ML expressions:
    (a) **(fn x => x)**
    (b) **(fn x => x x)**
    (c) **let exception E in raise E end**
    (d) **let val f = (fn x => x) in (f 3, f true) end**
    (e) **(fn f => (f 3, f true)) (fn x => x)**

28. Using the operating system dependent interface in SML of NJ, write a function
    find that gathers the names of all the files in the current directory matching a
    regular expression. Use the data structure for regular expressions from exercise 18
    and the string parser from exercise 20. An example use of **find** might look like
    the following:

    ML> find "*\\.c";
        ["prog.c"] : string list

29. Extend the previous exercise to examine all the files in the current directory and all
    the directories below the current one in the UNIX hierarchical file system. Add a
    new metasymbol, say **#**, to match any directory sequence $dir_1/dir_2/\cdots/dir_n$.

Glossary

algebraic data types (Page 71) A structured data type whose values are constructed using a given collection of constructors out of values of other types.

constructors (Page 39) Constructors are special data-creating functions important to pattern matching.

conventional languages (Page 2) A conventional programming language is one in which the primary means of computation is step-after-step execution and the assignment statement.

functional languages (Page 2) A functional programming language, as opposed to a conventional language, is one in which the primary means of computation is the function, not the assignment statement.

global binding (Page 32) A top-level binding is called a global binding.

higher-order functions (Page 60) A higher-order function is one that takes functions as arguments or returns functions as results.

lexical scoping (Page 50) In lexical scoping the values of free identifiers in functions are determined relative to the environment in which the function is defined. Most modern languages, including ML, use lexical scoping.

pattern (Page 38) A pattern is a term built from identifiers and constructors used to match against values.

polymorphism (Page 58) A function is said to be polymorphic when it works for elements of more than one type.

polytypes (Page 58) Type expressions containing type variables are called polytypes.

run-time stack (Page 99) At any instant during the execution of a program the set of currently pending subprograms is called the run-time stack.

session (Page 8) A session is an interactive dialog of phrase, response, phrase response, and so on with the ML system. It is terminated by typing a control-D.

short-circuit evaluation (Page 16) In short-circuit evaluation of operands of a binary, boolean operator, the operands are evaluated in order but only if necessary.

stream (Page 136) A stream is a sequence of data elements of indefinite length accessible one by one as each becomes available or is produced.

structured data types (Page 11) Structured data types are those data types composed of other data structures, as opposed to basic or primitive data types that cannot be broken into more fundamental data types.

terms (Page 143) Terms are expressions built out of variables and constants, and out of other terms using (uninterpreted) function symbols.

top level (Page 8) The level of direct interaction with the ML system. Usually indicated by some kind of prompt.

unification (Pages 119 and 143) Unification is the process of finding values of variables to make terms syntactically equal.

values (Page 29) The data objects that are manipulated by ML computations are called values.

Bibliography

[1] ANDREW W. APPEL and DAVID B. MACQUEEN. A standard ML compiler. In Gilles Kahn, editor, *Functional Programming Languages and Computer Architecture*, pages 301–324. Springer-Verlag, Berlin, 1987.

[2] LUCA CARDELLI. Basic polymorphic typechecking. *Science of Computer Programming*, 8(2):147–172, April 1987.

[3] LUCA CARDELLI. Typeful programming. Technical Report SRC Report 45, Digital Equipment Corporation, Systems Research Center, Palo Alto, CA, May 1989.

[4] LUIS DAMAS and ROBIN MILNER. Principal type-schemes for functional programs. In *Conference Record of the Ninth Annual ACM Symposium on Principles of Programming Languages*, pages 207–212. ACM, 1982.

[5] ANTHONY J. FIELD and PETER G. HARRISON. *Functional Programming*. Addison-Wesley, Wokingham, England, 1988.

[6] MICHAEL J. C. GORDON, ROBIN MILNER, and CHRISTOPHER P. WADSWORTH. *Edinburgh LCF*. Springer-Verlag, Berlin, 1979.

[7] CHARLES ANTONY RICHARD HOARE. Recursive data structures. *International Journal of Computer and Information Sciences*, 4(2):105–132, June 1975.

[8] BRUCE J. MACLENNAN. *Functional Programming: Practice and Theory*. Addison-Wesley, Reading, MA, 1990.

[9] HARRY G. MAIRSON. Deciding ML typability is complete for deterministic exponential time. In *Conference Record of the Seventeenth Annual ACM Symposium on Principles of Programming Languages*, pages 382–401. ACM, 1990.

[10] MICHEL MAUNY. Functional programming using CAML light. Technical report, INRIA, Le Chesnay, France, May 1991.

[11] ROBIN MILNER. A theory of type polymorphism in programming. *Journal of Computer and System Science*, 17(3):348–375, December 1978.

[12] ROBIN MILNER and MADS TOFTE. *Commentary on Standard ML*. MIT Press, Cambridge, MA, 1991.

[13] ROBIN MILNER, MADS TOFTE, and ROBERT HARPER. *The Definition of Standard ML*. MIT Press, Cambridge, MA, 1990.

[14] CHRIS READE. *Elements of Functional Programming*. Addison-Wesley, Wokingham, England, 1989.

[15] STEFAN SOKOŁOWSKI. *Applicative High Order Programming: The Standard ML Perspective*. Chapman & Hall Computing, London, 1991.

[16] MADS TOFTE. Four lectures on standard ML. Technical Report ECS-LFCS-89-73, Department of Computer Science, University of Edinburgh, March 1989.

[17] MADS TOFTE. Type inference for polymorphic references. *Information and Computation*, 89:1–34, November 1990.

[18] MITCHELL WAND. A simple algorithm and proof for type inference. *Fundamenta Informaticae*, 10(2):115–122, June 1987.

[19] DAVID ANTHONY WATT. Executable semantic descriptions. *Software–Practice and Experience*, 16(1):13–43, January 1986.

[20] ÅKE WIKSTRÖM. *Functional Programming Using Standard ML*. Prentice Hall, Englewood Cliffs, NJ, 1987.

Index